WESTLAKE

WESTLAKE

Poems by
Wayne Kaumualii Westlake
(1947–1984)

Wayne Kaumualii Westlake

Edited By
MEI-LI M. SIY and RICHARD HAMASAKI

Talanoa: Contemporary Pacific Literature
University of Hawai'i Press
Honolulu

Library of Congress Cataloging-in-Publication Data

Westlake, Wayne.

[Poems. Selections]

Westlake : poems by Wayne Kaumualii Westlake (1947–1984)
/ Wayne Kaumualii Westlake ; edited by Mei-Li M. Siy and Richard
Hamasaki.   p. cm. —

(Talanoa) Includes bibliographical references.

ISBN 978-0-8248-3067-0 (pbk. : alk. paper)

I. Siy, Mei-Li M. II. Hamasaki, Richard. III. Title. IV.
Series.

PS3623.E8495A6 2009

811'.6—dc22

2008040474

Designed by 'Elepaio Press

Contents

Wayne Kaumaulii Westlake, 1983 Poetry Reading at Heʻeia Kea, Oʻahu.

Preface

BY

Wayne Kaumualii Westlake (1947–1984)

My poems are autobiography—like poetic diary—moments immediately recorded that would otherwise have passed by unnoticed.

When I'm depressed, my poems give me strength to endure the absurd. If the words don't get you, then think of perception—what exactly is fit subject for poetry? I say everything—or nothing. Everything is poetry to me!

In writing poetry I've experimented with many forms—lately the form I've found most exciting is poetry diary form—short poems written to record fresh poetic insight (whatever that may mean). There's poetry all around us—we only have to open our eyes and see it—incidents, thoughts, feelings, experiences all grounded in everyday life—these are the flesh and bones of this poetry—recorded as they waste away.

I've been writing poems since I was 16—after writing for 5 years I burnt all my poems—5 years of sweat and blood, 10 minutes up in smoke—never burn your poems—you'll always regret it—anyway I've saved all the poems since.

I remember a friend, an old poet, saying out loud at a party when I walked in: "Watch-out, folks, he's reflective!" Well, (shiny) like a mirror, here I am.

For local-born artists, isolation has both its benefits and its drawbacks. Personally, I prefer the isolation for it offers me insulation from inundating outside influences. But every imu (oven) has its inside and its out, and the isolation I cherish and thrive on can have a devastating reverse effect when it comes to obtaining exposure outside of Hawaii for works conceived and produced in our unique environment.

[Editors' Note: This preface was excerpted and compiled from three separate, unpublished manuscripts.]

Self Portrait   10-25-81

Mark Hamasaki

1983 Poetry Reading Co-organized by Ilima Piianaia (1947–2006) at Heʻeia Kea, Oʻahu. Seated *(front row):* Cecilia Kapua Lindo, Haunani Bernardino (1949–2006), Tamara Wong-Morrison, Leialoha Apo Perkins, John Dominis Holt (1919–1993), Joe Balaz, Albert Wendt; *(back row):* Kalena Silva, Wayne Kaumualii Westlake (1947–1984), Kalani Akana, and Imaikalani Kalahele.

Introduction

In an all too brief life and literary career, Wayne Edward Kaumualii Miller Westlake (1947–1984) produced a substantial body of poetry consisting of hundreds of short poems and longer narrative pieces.[1] He broke new ground as a concrete poet, translated Taoist classical literature and Japanese haiku, interwove perspectives from his Hawaiian heritage into his writing and art, and indefatigably published his poetry in small presses and anthologies in Hawai'i and abroad. When Westlake died in Hilo Hospital on February 16, 1984, at the age of 36, two weeks after his car was struck by an allegedly drunken driver, the only available collection of his poems was a 32-page, limited edition chapbook from an independently published small press.[2] Long overdue, *Westlake* showcases one of contemporary Hawai'i's most versatile poets.

In 2001, seventeen years after Westlake's death, his former partner and present literary executor, Mei-Li M. Siy, gathered and organized many of his manuscripts and papers, which had been lying for years in boxes, stored in a shed near her family home in Hawai'i. Receiving these unpublished poems and manuscripts from Mei-Li initiated a deeply emotional journey—for both of us—to document and honor his life and work.[3] *Westlake* includes published and unpublished poetry, composed from the late 1960s to 1984, by one whose talents have yet to be fully appreciated and studied. This is a poet who worked and struggled in an era when few authors from Hawai'i, particularly those of Hawaiian ancestry, had access to established presses.

According to Wayne's brother Ward, their Hawaiian genealogical line flows from mother Elsa Marjorie Reichardt and maternal grandmother Jane Miller, originally from Maui. Elsa, who earned a master's degree from Columbia University, documented the brothers' genealogy that "goes back to the king of Kauai" [Kaumuali'i].[4] Their German ancestry came from their father, Frank Raymond Westlake, formerly of Kaua'i.[5] Ward believed that Wayne learned of his Hawaiian name while attending a private academy, Punahou School in Honolulu, when "they needed their Hawaiian names for the Holokū Ball." According to Ward, Kaumualii was Wayne's given name, established from his mother's research and validated by a family relative or close family friend. Wayne began including Kaumualii as part of his name in the mid-1970s when he initiated a letter-writing campaign addressing cultural issues and Hawaiian land struggles.

After his ashes were secreted near Kīlauea in a ceremony organized by Mei-Li and two of his friends, Palikapu Dedman and Emmett Aluli, Wayne's brothers and father held a second funeral at the Diamond Head Memorial Park. His memorial plaque reads "Wayne Edward Westlake." Westlake used many pen names from as early as 1972: Kamalii Kahewai (for his unpublished series "Down on the Sidewalk in Waikiki"); Edward Kaumualii (in the periodical *Writer's Ink*); Wayne Kaumualii Westlake; Wayne K. Westlake, and Wayne Westlake. Westlake once confided that his mother was initially perturbed by and had admonished him against using his "kapu name," Kaumualii, in his editorials.[6] Despite this, he refused either to yield or to shield his Hawaiian name; the cultural and political stakes were too high, especially regarding issues related to identity that he addressed during this last decade of his life.

Westlake was born in Lāhaina, Maui, in 1947 and his family moved to ʻĀina Haina, Oʻahu, when he was in elementary school. Later, all four brothers, William, Wayne, Ward, and Wendell, attended Punahou on athletic scholarships, and each excelled in football and other sports—their high school athletic achievements are well documented in Honolulu newspapers throughout the 1960s. Ward and several of Wayne's childhood friends confirmed stories of Wayne's athleticism, charisma, and rebelliousness. And while neither his friends nor Ward could remember Wayne ever revealing a high school interest in composing poetry, Ward felt that Wayne's creativity probably started at Punahou, where he was always a "good student who played lots of sports" and nearly always earned "good grades."[7] Russell Kokubun, Wayne's friend since elementary school, remembered that Wayne, in his youth, had earned a reputation as an artist. This talent would emerge in his concrete poetry, in various collages published in the literary magazine *Ramrod,* edited by Joe Balaz, and in sketches of threatened Hawaiian petroglyphs that he discovered on Kahoʻolawe when it was occupied and used as a target island by the U.S. military.

After graduating from Punahou in 1966, Westlake attended the University of Oregon and began, in earnest, his lifelong study of world literatures. The earliest poems included in *Westlake* were compiled in Oregon, probably sometime shortly before or after he dropped out of college in 1969. He often spoke of a teacher and poet in Eugene who was affiliated with a group called "Yesterday's Onion" and of another teacher who drew Westlake toward Asian languages, art and poetry, sake drinking, and tea. Bo Hunter, a close friend of Westlake's from Hawai'i who stayed with him in Eugene from December 1970 to May 1971, recalled that eventually Westlake could "go head to head with all of the professors of Chinese literature and philosophy there, quitting school after there were no more Asian literature or history classes to take." Westlake's transition from college student to college dropout in Oregon initiated a long period when he independently studied classical Chinese, poetry, philosophy, and all aspects of Taoism, as well as a plethora of world authors.[8]

An early poem (circa 1972) reveals Westlake incorporating aspects of Taoist philosophy into his own evolving Hawaiian aesthetic and political consciousness. He wrote:

taoist hawaiian

someone yells:
HEAD'S UP!—
i put my head
down
good thinking—eh?

In an ancient feudalistic war-torn China, philosophers Chuang Tzu, Mencius, Lao Tzu (4th century B.C.), and other Taoist poets, particularly of the T'ang dynasty (618 to 907 A.D.), informed Westlake of philosophies that aligned well with his Hawaiian traditions: "The Taoist wayfarers were heirs to several sources of most ancient knowledge: shamans who knew how to alter consciousness; curers who studied the properties of plants and minerals; diviners who studied the weather, the stars, the animals, and the balance of the environment as a whole ... chieftains and courts of high antiquity who laid the groundwork of civilization; court scribes and historians, whose work confronted them daily with the moral and political lessons of the ages."[9] One of Westlake's early translations of poet Han Shan (circa 8th century) evokes Taoist symbolism alluding to understanding and enlightenment:

Footprints of the Ancients left on thousand year-old stones
In front of ten-thousand cliffs—one spot empty
Here always the bright Moon shines pure and clear
Never bothering to ask East or West![10]

In a short poem that appeared in the same issue featuring his Han Shan translations, Westlake declares: "East / I'm afraid / does not / meet West— / they COLLIDE!" Unlike poet Han Shan, East and West did matter to Westlake, particularly in the Pacific Islands region—with Oceania either caught in the middle of conflicts between East and West or forever relegated to a cultural and political periphery. Westlake had immersed himself in works spanning from Sun Tzu's *Art of War* (circa 400–320 B.C.) to Mao Tse-tung's *On Literature and Art* (1960), and he was, for example, well versed in strategies of war and insurgency that were effectively implemented by Mao Tse-tung against those who tried to destroy the Communists in their struggle to free China from foreign domination. Westlake's nontraditional, primarily self-taught education in the literary arts focused on work far beyond any western literary canon. This background not only nurtured an eclectic aesthetic, but fully prepared him to adapt strategies and principles by which to write on behalf of not widely known or even unpopular Hawaiian- and Pacific Islands-related issues in the late 1970s and early 1980s—a Taoist Hawaiian, indeed.

Inspired by his readings and bolstered by antiwar movements in the U.S., Westlake would soon experience a harsh wake-up call. In the late 1960s, at the height of the Vietnam War, after he had dropped out of the University of Oregon and while he was still living in Eugene, Westlake's draft notice arrived—unbeknownst to him—at his mother's home in Hawai'i. Ward recalled that his mother informed Wayne of its arrival, and after learning that her son was unequivocally opposed to the war, she "decided to support her son one-hundred percent." Mrs. Elsa Westlake hired an attorney to help Wayne apply for conscientious objector status in Honolulu. Ward remembered that Wayne flew home, where he locked himself in his bedroom with "no food or water" and the only noise that came from the room was the sound of his typewriter—for three days. Wayne finally emerged with a lengthy statement that so impressed Elsa's attorney that he offered to represent Wayne pro bono. Wayne was eventually granted conscientious objector status. Ironically, according to his friends from high school, Westlake had excelled in the ROTC program that was mandatory for male sophomores and juniors at Punahou. In contrast, his experiences in Oregon had helped to draw a line between the study of war and war itself. The "art of war," its stratagems and philosophies, particularly espoused by Sun Tzu, Che Guevara, Ho Chi Minh, and Mao Tse-tung, would remain with him for a lifetime and inform his poetry and political writings.

After spending nearly five years away from home, with only occasional trips back to Hawai'i, Westlake returned for good in late 1971 or early 1972. Initially, he lived in his family home in 'Āina Haina, back then a sleepy East Honolulu suburb, from which he walked to school and work, earning his income as a janitor in Waikīkī while pursuing his B.A. in Chinese studies at the University of Hawai'i.[11] He also spent time in Mānoa in the "temple," a traditional Chinese shrine and annex within the family home of his childhood friend Myron Wong, an informal gathering place for a handful of Westlake's closest companions from his middle and high school years. During the next decade, Westlake produced the bulk of his extant poems.

When I first met Westlake in late 1974 in Mānoa, O'ahu, at a reception for a visiting poet, he was relaxed yet intense and gracious. He could be quiet and moody, but once engaged would grow animated and expansive. As I was five years his junior, there was much for me to learn from and admire about Westlake's convictions, literary devotions, and life experiences. In 1975, we began teaching in the Poets in the Schools Program, and a year later, with mutual friends and colleagues, began collaborating on a literary magazine, *Seaweeds and Constructions,* published on a meager income but nurtured by a collective vision to integrate art and literature locally, regionally, and internationally.[12]

Westlake was also active in reading poetry, including his translations, and in promoting writing by locally born authors and students. His public readings were as diverse as his published works; on one occasion, he read Han Shan translations with poets Wing Tek Lum and Michael Among (a.k.a., "black dog"). In the mid-1970s, he read translations of Issa on KTUH-FM when Eric Chock and I moderated "Haku Mele o Hawai'i." When Westlake read from his Poets in the Schools student compilations, "Born Pidgin" and "Kahoolawe—Chants, Legends, Poems, Stories by Children of Maui," he would easily make the transition from English to Pidgin (Hawai'i Creole English) and back. His public appearances reflected the many personae of his wide-ranging poems, his voice clear, paced, and voluminous. At times, he'd evoke a deadpan tone with his polemic satires or reveal raw, trembling emotion when speaking publicly about the conflicts he had with former board members of the Hawai'i Literary Arts Council or with others whom he felt were giving undue preference to authors from the U.S. continent at the expense of talented poets, artists, and musicians from Hawai'i.

Westlake engaged in conversations and maintained relationships on a variety of levels, and he moved comfortably in circles that rarely intersected—Pidgin-speaking coworkers, family members, peers, and professionals. He was generous to his friends and compassionate to others more needy than he, despite deriving his modest income mostly as a laborer—a janitor, a construction worker at various O'ahu job sites, and, for a long stint, a baggage handler for Continental Airlines. He was a big-wave body surfer and at one point trained to enter bodysurfing contests on O'ahu, but after much deliberation decided to surf only for enjoyment. Some of his poems document heady nights of carousing, drinking, and smoking, but as his manuscripts testify, he lived and breathed poetry, his hands never far from any available scrap of paper that he could scribble on.

From the mid-1970s, while working at Continental Airlines, Westlake used his limited travel benefits to fulfill his dream of visiting Asia, but his trips were brief, and as the Hawaiian sovereignty movement gained momentum, he became increasingly involved in issues that impacted Oceania. Despite elements of impartiality in some of his editorials, Westlake believed unequivocally in a separatist relationship regarding any future demarcations between Hawai'i and the United States. This period marked a time when he turned to journalism to draw attention to land struggles in Hawai'i, issues of sovereignty, and a nuclear-free Pacific.[13] Early evidence of Westlake's editorial writing surfaced in two letters to the editor in 1968 and 1969; however, he published most of his articles and editorials in the late 1970s to early 1980s—in the daily papers *Honolulu Advertiser* and the *Honolulu Star-Bulletin*, in the independent news magazine *Hawaii Observer*, in *Pacific Islands Monthly*, Alu Like's *The Native Hawaiian*, the Socialist *Ka Huliau*, and Hilo's *Hawaii Tribune-Herald*.[14]

Teaching part-time in the Poets in the Schools program significantly shaped his perspectives, but the work was sporadic, averaging only 15 hours a week per school, perhaps at just three or four schools a year. In February 1977, two years after Westlake began teaching in the Poets in the

Schools program, George Helm, Hawaiian leader of the Protect Kahoʻolawe ʻOhana, and his companion Kimo Mitchell mysteriously disappeared at sea. They and a surviving companion, Billy Mitchell (no relation to Kimo), had secretly landed on Kahoʻolawe in search of their friends, Walter Ritte and Richard Sawyer, Jr., who had spent two weeks eluding the U.S. Navy in protest and in defiance against the military, which was using the island as a bombing range.[15] Ritte and Sawyer were arrested by the U.S. military on Kahoʻolawe in July 1977. Helm and Mitchell's deaths and Ritte and Sawyer's incarceration affected Westlake deeply, and soon afterward he compiled and self-published a collection of poems, "Kahoolawe—Chants, Legends, Poems, Stories by the Children of Maui," written by elementary school students who were enrolled in his Poets in the Schools classes.[16] A local printer donated paper, including cover stock; Mikihala (Ah Chan) Among typed the stencils; and Bob Matsuda, then director of the Nuʻuanu YMCA, where I worked part-time as a desk clerk on the swing shift, gave us permission to mimeograph copies in the administrative office on a predetermined weekend. Once they had been compiled, Westlake personally distributed copies to legislators at the State Capitol in 1977.[17] Not only did he produce significant, creative indictments condemning the U.S. Navy's bombardment of Kahoʻolawe, but in November 1977, as a reporter for the *Hawaii Observer*, he published a penetrating interview conducted with Hawaiian political prisoners Richard Sawyer and Walter Ritte, Jr. Both had been incarcerated since July 29 of that same year for occupying Kahoʻolawe while desperately struggling to protect the island from further desecration.[18]

On July 18, 1979, the *Honolulu Star-Bulletin* announced that Westlake had discovered about 30 Hawaiian petroglyphs on the then target island of Kahoʻolawe, where he had spent ten days as a volunteer assisting in an archeological study with the Protect Kahoʻolawe ʻOhana "searching the northeastern tip of the Island." The reporter described Westlake's concerns: "Westlake said the nature of the petroglyphs suggests that a civilization made that area its permanent home. 'The petroglyphs tell stories, illustrate activities, document events and praise the gods. . . . They indicate habitation, civilization, culture and spirituality.'" Westlake described to the reporter that "the petroglyphs were weathered, hard to see and crumbling from heat and salt air. They were so fragile, he said, that he didn't dare try to make rubbings, but copied them in a series of sketches instead."[19] Westlake's hand-drawn petroglyphs from Kahoʻolawe, as well as his research and theories regarding the significance of ancient Hawaiian rock carvings and figures, would appear in various publications in Hawai'i and else-where. He also published images of Kaho'olawe's petroglyphs in his Poets in the Schools lesson plans.[20] Such action reflected a growing cultural and literary activism on Westlake's part, and he was determined to introduce, beyond mere tokenism, a significant body of Hawai'i's literature into the classroom. Toward that end, in 1980 Westlake and I cofounded a course for the Ethnic Studies Program at the University of Hawai'i at Mānoa that featured literatures produced by indigenous and nonindigenous authors, poets, composers, and playwrights from Hawai'i.[21]

Westlake once wrote, in *Haku Mele o Hawaii*, a Poets in the Schools publication, that "The role of the teacher is not so much to teach any particular subject, but to teach learning itself. By exciting the children's natural curiosity they will learn just about anything by themselves."[22] His friends can still vividly recall seeing Westlake's slow-gesturing arms, his intensely serious face, with trembling lower lip and quivering hands, when he discussed his discoveries on Kaho'olawe as if the spirit of the land itself were speaking through him. For Westlake, his indigenous ancestors themselves were embodied within Kaho'olawe's endangered petroglyphs—ancient rock carvings that offered and needed protection, in perpetuity.

From the late 1970s to his death in 1984, Westlake's writing continued to bridge literary traditions as he expanded his reach beyond Hawai'i's shores. For example, he published—in Japan and Canada—English translations by the nineteenth-century haiku poet Issa. After "Manifesto" (for Concrete Poetry) and a corresponding new series of work were published in Hawai'i in 1979, he sought larger audiences for his concrete poems and, in an unusual move, convinced small-press editors to reprint these and other previously published poems in magazines and literary journals from San Francisco to New York to London to Madras.[23] Westlake's literary wayfaring reveals many routes, as he navigated through poetic forms and philosophies, reshaping his work, often exploring and experimenting with what he called "absurdism." In one of his letters, written from Volcano in 1981, he enclosed three poems about his dog, a German Shepard named Kona. "I expect that you might think this is ridiculous, writing poems about my dog but I'm an advocate of absurdism and writing poems about my dog in this day and age is absurdist at best . . . I've written three poems here: 'Sending My Dog to College' 'On Having An Intelligent Conversation with My Dog' and 'My Dog is Panting.' . . . Three more coming up: 'My Boy is a Coconut Boy' 'The Name of My Dog's Dog Food Is My Name.' . . . And maybe the last one is 'God is Dog Spelled Backwards.'"[24] Westlake's "absurdism" flows throughout his work, his writing reflecting "everything" he observed that amused or struck him. This apprehension of the absurd connects seamlessly with the epigrammatic qualities of brief, reflective poems that he developed through his study of many literary masters.

Westlake was determined to gain recognition as a poet in his own lifetime, but like the personae within his work, he never took himself too seriously. Time and again, his efforts to publish his ever-growing stack of poetry manuscripts were set aside so he could help others publish and read publicly. He also devoted hours preparing for public testimony related to Hawaiian land struggles and controversies associated with the arts in Hawai'i. Nor did his status as an outspoken contemporary native Hawaiian writer help him in his campaign against ignorance and the suppression of indigenous artists and authors by educators and publishers in Hawai'i and elsewhere.[25] In a 1980 letter to the editor titled "Hawaiian Artists' Plight," he wrote:

> Unfortunately, in the arts community of Hawaii, the missionary ideal still prevails. Like the missionaries, the government art "experts" have deeply ingrained in their souls the ludicrous belief that the art world of Hawaii is so backward and behind the times that artists from all over the world have a moral mission to bring the saving artistic light to us pagan artists of Hawaii. Their god of art lives in New York, Paris or Japan. And there is no other god of art but theirs.
>
> Where that leaves us, the savage artists of Hawaii, is starving in the dark. Which incidentally, in our religion, is the naked source of all life, light and art.[26]

Westlake had reached a crossroads. In 1981, he and his companion Mei-Li M. Siy moved to the island of Hawai'i. Westlake's creative output slowed considerably as he devoted substantial time to researching and testifying against geothermal development in Puna and against a hotly contested proposal to build a rocket and satellite launching facility in Ka'ū. He and Mei-Li finally settled in a modest house located in an isolated rain forest on Jade Street, only a few miles from the 1983 eruption that continues to flow to this day.

In 1983, with encouragement and support from Marjorie Tuainekore Crocombe, Subramani and Albert Wendt who, at the time, were teaching at the University of the South Pacific (Fiji campus), we coproduced our seventh and last issue of *Seaweeds and Constructions*.[27] This final issue, *A Pacific Islands Collection*, anthologized previously published authors from Oceania and juxtaposed their writing with work by artists from Hawai'i, a collaboration that would eventually lead to unprecedented networking between indigenous artists and authors of Hawai'i and their counterparts throughout Oceania. A year later, Westlake was dead. Devastated, the main circle of writers and artists involved in producing *Seaweeds and Constructions* ended the series after a final 1984 reprinting of this same issue, dedicated to his memory.[28]

While memories of Westlake continue to elicit tears, laughter, and warm head-shaking smiles among his friends and companions, *Westlake* revives, for a wider audience, the expansive spirit of the man who lives within his poems, chronicling an inventive poetic journey significantly infused by a wide-ranging passion for world and indigenous literatures. Assuming many poetic personae, always resisting naïveté, vanity, and injustice, Westlake's reflections are as diverse as Hawai'i's multiethnic populations yet are always grounded in his intense commitment to the land and culture of his native Hawaiian ancestors.

Prepare to be provoked!

Richard Hamasaki
Kāne'ohe, 2007

WESTLAKE

the
POEMS

A Joke—To Tu Fu
After Li Po

On top Puff-Rice Mountain I meet Tu Fu!
Wearing a bamboo rain-hat in the noonday sun!
I ask, since parting, how come so thin?
Suffering from poetry, again?

my poems—

something hiding here

WAYNE WESTLAKE
(you ask?)
sitting
walking
lying down

WHO?

just like naupaka
i'm half
in the mountains
half
by the sea

taoist hawaiian

someone yells:
HEAD'S UP!—
i put my head
down
good thinking—eh?

everyone needs
    a place to go
sometime and contemplate
       the everlasting sadness
   of life.

i found one
      in a chinese temple
way back in manoa

to the spirit of ishikawa takuboku

more sad
than the cherry
blossoms blown
in the spring wind—
a poet
dying young

dish
dish
dish
dish
dish
dish
dish
dish
dish
dish
dish
dish
dish
dish
dish
dish
dish
dish
dish
dish
dish
dish
dish
dish

          m
    s   a   h e
              s   d

            i
       d   s
               he
                  s

spring wind
      nothing to blow
this bald head!

thinking of home

here in oregon
with nothing to do
i wish i had
    some sushi

snow

thick morning fog
the sun frozen
a small white ball

the naked child
pats the stream rocks
'hee—hee—hee!'

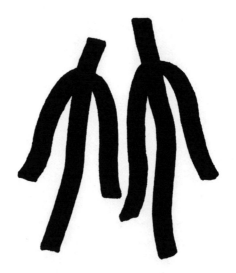

BAMBOOS

o! o!
   spring bamboo
battered
     by the hail!

Look at these fine nuts—
that's what the squirrel said
high in the trees.

eating soy beans
one by one throwing off dirty thoughts
the diamond brilliance
brightens

eh—you
don't give me
any of your
acid enlightenment
you just dropped
even deeper in
darkness

Spring:

  The weeds in bloom—

O I'm happy!

LINDA'S POEMS

The gods in the sky
reveal themselves
in clouds

                                    Wind watching
                                      the trees, the seas
                                          and me

            Hairless mountains
            lifeless streams

                                          trees, trees!
                                            trees,
                                                cut.

WOMAN'S LIBERATION

 = woman under roof = peace, contentment
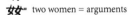= woman with child = goodness
妆= two women = arguments

21

such different thoughts
the cat and me
watching the bird

amazed!
i stepped in dog shit
viewing the cherry blossoms

"it's simple, it's simple!"
said the frog—
then silence

deep in the forest
a man lives
in a tree stump

please, please!
leave the leaves
alone

it's only the sound of water in the gutter
then how come
      i'm so thrilled?

hanging the picture
i gaze instead
at the moon

the moon and the cross

their light

is not the same

DRINKING WINE
—poems of the Tao

(1)

winter spring summer fall
naturally make a year—
outside the dust and noise
what's the use of wisdom?
drifting in the wind
the floating cloud returns—
at death
t'ao chi'en's only regret
he didn't drink enough

light the pipe! pass the cups!
you'll die too

(2)

five cups of rice
two bottles of wine
long past midnight
drunk!
laughing!

passing out in the pavilion—
drink lots of sake
then try laugh

(3)

cold sake rots the brain
hot sake gets you high
cup after cup
'three cups—penetrate the TAO!'
pass the cups!
'never refuse a drink!'

(4)

winter pushes summer
night chases day
sit back—grow old
have another cup
let it change

nothing to lose—
once you get this
no more hurry

(5)

day eating night
night eating day
all i can do is laugh!

(6)

t'ao ch'ien lived near cars and trucks
yet never heard the noise—
how so?
drunk! in the wine pavillion
gazing at the moon!

(7)

a madman? a fool?
i laugh a lot—
you ever tasted
a dew drop?

Sitting on Chao-chou

wu!
wu!
wu!
wu!
wu!
wu!
wu!
wu!
wu!
wu!
wu!
wu!
wu!
wu!
wu!
wu!
wu!
wu!
wu!
wu!
wu!
wu!
wu!
wu!
wu!
wu!
wu!
wu!
wu!
wu!
wu!
wu!
wu!
wu!
wu!
wu!

Looks of disbelief:
I'm on my knees
Washing a rock.

mind like wood
    sunset feels good
on this bald head

the morning was quiet
until outside
someone started screaming
god! god! god! god!

birth
decay
sickness
pain
death
sorrow
sadness
despair

—buddha never lied

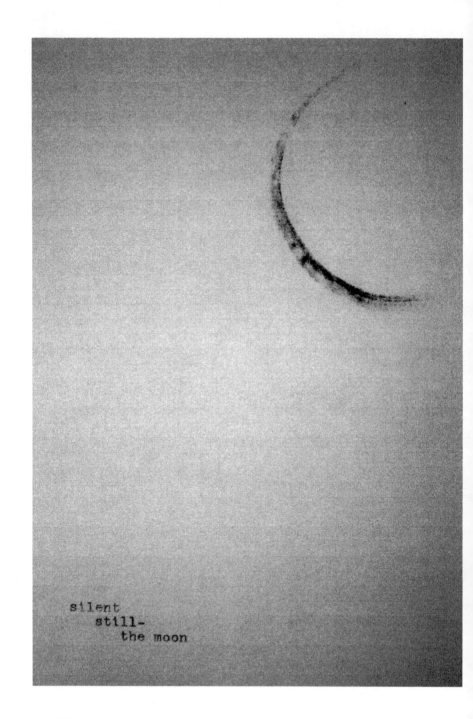

silent
   still-
      the moon

never stop

madness! madness!
too much tea!
fill the cup!
fill the bowl!
madness! madness!
too much tea!

cats don't care
   trampling flowers
chasing the white
     spring butterfly

quietly up
    the rocky trail
   I'm walking
       to the moon!

               motor cars, people in a hurry
                  somewhere below
                     these clouds.

poets lie dead
    on library shelves
'in the book of Immortals
    they all are nameless.'

cockroach

with the money

    i got for

        christmas,

i buy my self

        some Kafka—

IDIOTS!

    i crawl out of

        the bookstore

        like a cockroach!

Stars, then clouds
stars, then clouds
all night long.

Bald head
No shirt, no pants—
  Good summer clothes!

watching cats play
this silly grin
stuck on my face

Full moon—
    hibiscus bark
        tastes like rain . . .

Gonna check
    all my pockets
for what I don't know . . .

KLAMATH FALLS

"A transient, who was found lying
along railroad tracks west of Klamath
Falls, died . . . He apparently
fell from a moving train near Midlands"

Harold L. McGrath, 45
was once a great, great man

when he died
no one cared
no one cried

unseen by the world
blood tears dripping
dripping from my heart.

the moon is round
the sun is round
the earth is round

the white man
made the indians
live in square houses

the indians died.

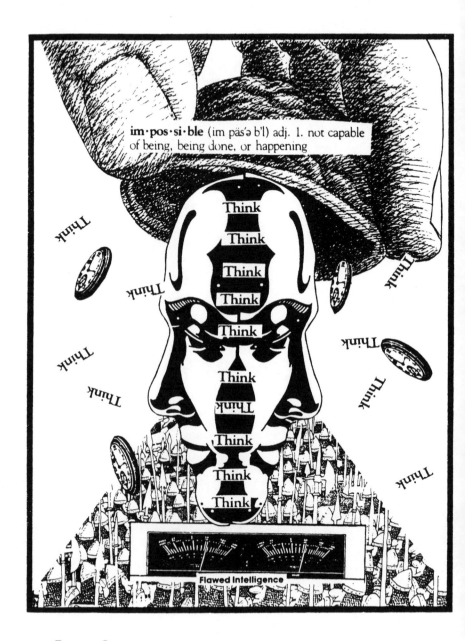

FLAWED INTELLIGENCE

48

Brittle Bones

sixty six
              to seventy two
man, it burned
              me out

how 'bout you

in a dream

the rains are warm
            here in Kalalau
      green everywhere

PAPAYAS! MANGOS!
I'M COMING HOME!
GUAVA! LYCHEE!
I'M COMING HOME!

SUSHI!
SUSHI!
I'M COMING HOME!

HAWAIIANS
EAT
FISH
EAT
HAWAIIANS
EAT
FISH
EAT
HAWAIIANS
EAT
FISH
EAT
HAWAIIANS
EAT
FISH

Ha

eighteen hundred
dead in nicaragua
and life in waikiki
goes on the same

janitor on his
    way to work
walking alone
        fine rain

four bus loads
full of tourists
i give each face
the bodhidharma stare.

Grandfather Was a Strange Man

my grandfather was a strange man:
an old-time intellectual, a german
runaway, steamship stowaway to
mexico then legged it to frisco
then freightshiped across the sea to
lahaina, maui. . . . i mean
my grandfather was a strange man;
he worked the sugar plantation
a luna, but not a brutal nazi like
so many—no i said
my grandfather was a strange man:
he married a hawaiian even, unheard
of then—a dirty hawaiian—a HEATHEN!
and he let me run around naked
in the Sun and insisted my hair grow
long and blond, like 'gorgeous george' . . .

my grandfather was a strange man:
he'd laugh a lot—just a baby we'd ride
the cane trains all over beautiful maui;
ah the good old days!—retired he'd listen
to the radio, news of his dying years—
his nose bled one day and wouldn't stop—
he didn't say much, smoked a lot
and died frosted white, like a neon light
in a hospital, somewhere in honolulu,
skin and bones, wasted—i took the phone

call from the hospital and knew and handed
the phone to my mother: i knew it first—
my grandpa died. . . .

my grandfather was a strange man:
at the funeral it was strange—
everyone was crying (no one knew him)
and i so young just stood there staring
at the gravemound and knew, ULTIMATELY
and FINALLY: i'd never see my grandpa
again—'so this is where the long road
ends?' too young, i learned the TRUTH . . .

my grandfather was a strange man:
i think about him by the stormy sea
twenty years later—still wearing his
old worn shirt—torn, ragged, threadbare—
held together with coconut leaf—

my grandfather was a strange man;
his old shirt still keeps me warm . . .

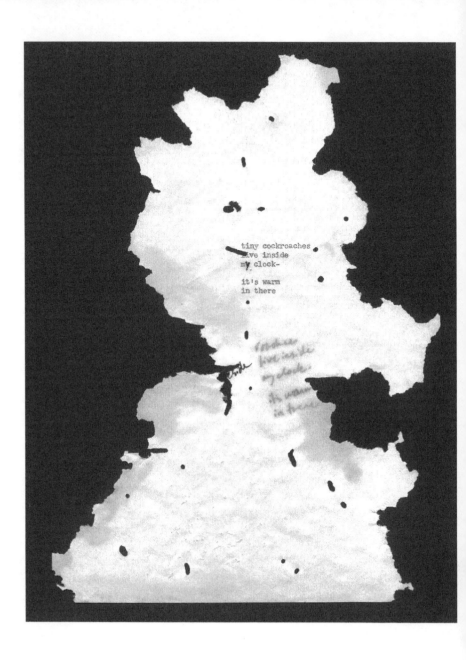

tiny cockroaches
live inside
my clock-

it's warm
in there

someone died
this spring—
no young people
at the funeral.

Realizing I'm a German

realizing i'm a german
                    hawaiian,
              and understanding
i have a tradition
                    of literature
              and ocean
behind me—
              gives me
              STRENGTH
                    as i stumble
insanely
        down the long
              deserted beach—
              wondering:
what
      am
          i
              doing
        here?

o there's something
wrong with that
              guy he's some
          kind of writer, a
collector
      of shells,
a beach bum
even—
          wise guy!
                    no,
he's just a poet!

stopping to rest
after the rain
i throw off
my pancho
like a cape
drop my walking
stick on the sand
i find a soft
coconut leaf
and fix up my
long gone
grandfather's shirt:
it's ragged, full
of holes—now
and threadbare
but
it still keeps
me warm when
the buttons
are all on . . .

realizing i'm a german
                hawaiian,
        i tear off my
     grandfather's shirt
and dive headfirst into
                the SEA!

in a dream

little old man
        planting rice
kept saying
  'come back
        tomorrow'

WATER A COW DRINKS TURNS TO VENOM

WATER A SNAKE DRINKS TURNS MILK

on the bus

rich lady
    on the bus
talk talk talk
        can't stop

i light a
    communist cigarette

big hit—
    let it out
        loud.

How's It Feel, Big Men?

HA!
all the People
            already at work
and there's still
            DEW left
                        on the grass . . .

i soak my feet in it
squinting in the sun

                        how's it feel,
Big Men?

OUT LIVED
            BY THE DEW!

the Sun rising
behind an island—
i swallow the Sun
and dive into
            the Sea!

ah!
it's cold
i'm cold
and there's seaweed
            in my hair!

i don't care
I DON'T CARE!
                        HA!
HERE COMES ANOTHER
                        WAVE!

and just like tigers
they caged us
          all in zoos
i can't stand it
how about you?

PUPULE

Ancient Stone

the girl i've
been staying with
starts her Cadillac.

i wait
in the shade
examining an ancient stone.

aah big grassy field
take off slippers
walk across
cold dew between
                my toes.

Felt Like Walking

nowhere to go
nothing to do
mindless i walked
and got there

second day
        at school
    just decided
i don't want
        to look at books
    want to look
            at clouds

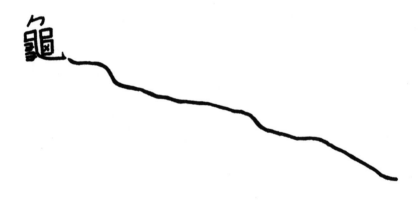

SACRED TORTOISE DRAGGING ITS ASS IN THE MUD

in the men's room
        at U.H.
people stop
        and wonder
in the sink
      bald head maniac
washing grapes.

slaving over books
   should be
      out raging
chinese characters
      driving me crazy
when will i
      ever learn?

writing characters
must be a million
what a relief
look up
          at Trees!

Dragon

a few times

'have you ever

             lived?'

        she asked—

'yeah'

    i told her,

'a few times.'

even DEATH

has exits

like a dark

theater

Some Critic Tried To Put Me Down

some critic put me down
"your poems lack meaning
you think you're important"
Ha!—he's crazy
i just had to laugh
'not anyone can read
        brush strokes of blood
the meaning being no meaning'

A Thousand Poems

. . . and life goes on
by

blurring

nobody loves
          a loser

there are gods
but no

      GOD

one of the hardest
       things
          to do
in the world
         is to eat rice
with chop
     sticks
   off a
     plate!

a poet needs
     ENCOURAGEMENT
sometimes or else
    the ABSUR
        DITY of
   it all
can OVER
    WHELM
      him . . .

late at night
all alone
like a treasure chest
i open my suitcase
full of neatly
piled poems

namuamidabutsu

the bug
     i sliced
with my cane-
               knife
on its back
rubbing its legs
          like praying
     for mercy.

you ever heard of
     mercy
          killing?

i chop the bugger
in half
"namuamidabutsu
once for you
namuamidabutsu
once for me"

Penniless Poet

penniless
starving
nothing to eat
      for weeks
i stumble
      around the house
   from room
       to room
    to room
in stinking socks!

hermit crab
i compliment you
your fine taste
in choosing
a house

at the beach
   a tourist asks
'how many people
killed by the waves
      each week?'
i just laugh
  'thousands'

'ō'ō 'ō'ō

'ō'ō 'ō'ō

'ō'ō 'ō'ō

'ō'ō 'ō'ō

'ō'ō 'ō'ō

'ō'ō 'ō'ō

'ō'ō 'ō'ō

ō ō

'ō'ō

W. Westlake '79

sitting by
    the waterfall
at night

first thing
    after meditation

scratch all
    the mosquito bites

penny's found
        a penny earned—
it's no empty
            saying

stack 'em up
    one neat pile
fifteen buys you
    one sushi

back door

sneaking out
  her back door
  in the morning
  i'm lucky
      to find
a sky
  full of stars

old man
farts out loud
no one around
but his
wife.

tiny bird
what are you doing
flying
    so high
here alone
    in these
        cold mountains?

the poet's trip

clenched fists—

i squeeze another
poem out
of my mind

SIHANOUK CALLS NIXON A LIAR
(on the death of W. C. Williams)

poets can't buy poetry:
how can they?
if they can buy poetry
they're not poets!

i sit on the cold
linoleum floor
in the back of
ala moana
center bookstore
reading william
carlos williams . . .

if i wrote poems
like this
they wouldn't give me
the pulitzer prize—
the book?
$2.95!

crazy man
the poems so good
and my money
just about out
i get up
and BUY
the book!
some poet, huh?
FOOL!
i'm ashamed
carrying around
a book!

books books books
lately been eating
books books books

bite
chew
swallow
spit out

bite
chew
swallow
spit out

books books books
lately been eaten by
books books books

bite
chew
swallow
disappear

Japanese Poets

shinkichi takahashi
takahashi shinkichi

ishikawa takuboku
takuboku ishikawa

hagiwara sakutaro
sakutaro hagiwara

japanese poets
i repeat their names
like poems
walking home alone

Red Light

if a guy
        has to impress
his girlfriend,
by going
        thru
                a red light,

he must not
        be able to
impress her,
alone
        in bed
                all night!

. . . and if a girl
        is impressed
by her boyfriend,
going
        thru
                a red light,

why she
        deserves everything
she doesn't get,
alone
        in bed
                all night!

you ought to be ashamed
twenty five years
still no enlightenment

DELIRIOUS – PATHOL.
WILD WITH EX-
CITEMENT.

DELIRIUM – PATHOL. – A MORE OR
LESS
TEMPORARY DISORDER
OF THE MENTAL FACULTIES,
AS IN FEVERS, DISTUR-
BANCES OF CONCIOUSNESS OR
IN TOXIFICATION.

DE LIRIUM TREMENS - PATHOL.
VIOLENT RESTLESSNESS
DUE TO EXCESSIVE & PROLONGED USE
OF ALCOHOL,
CHARACTERIZED BY
TREMBLING,
TERRIFYING
VISIONS.

Poet's Dictionary

97

down at school

flunked bad
        the history test
i wasn't expecting
i stare down at
my filthy wet feet

the persimmons
     i got
from the japanese store
          garbage

gave 'em to my
          chinese teacher
     today—

what could i say

couldn't tell the truth
     had to lie
     told him
          they're from lanai.

Lost Slippers—Cum Laude

Iron men
      in glass jars
sneak around
      selling names
and dates—
Blind People
it's GRADUATION DAY!

straight A's
HA!
FOOLED 'EM AGAIN!

lost slippers
cum laude
i'm graduating
from college
with HONORS
and i don't even
wear shoes!

LAUGH
LAUGH
i accept the diploma
GLADLY
and right there
on center stage
tear it up
INSANE!

no money
and i'm hungry
check my pocket
just in case

have to laugh
nothing there
of course

OOZING

o o o o o o o o o o o o o o o o o o o o o o o o o o o o o o
o o o o o o o o o o o o o o o o o o o o o o o o o o o o o o
o o o o o o o o o o o o o o o o o o o o o o o o o o o o o o
o o o o o o o o o o o o o o o o o o o o o o o o o o o o o o
o o o o o o o o o o o o o o o o o o o o o o o o o o o o o o
o o o o o o o o o o o o o o o o o o o o o o o o o o o o o o
o o o o o o o o o o o o o o o o o o o o o o o o o o o o o o
o o o o o o o o o o o o o o o o o o o o o o o o o o o o o o
o o o o o o o o o o o o o o o o o o o o o o o o o o o o o o
o o o o o o o o o o o o o o o o o o o o o o o o o o o o o o
o o o o o o o o o o o o o o o o o o o o o o o o o o o o o o
o o o o o o o o o o o o o o o o o o o o o o o o o o o o o o
o o o o o o o o o o o o o o o o o o o o o o o o o o o o o o
z z z z z z z z z z z z z z z z z z z z z z z z z z z z z
i i i i i i i i i i i i i i i i i i i i i i i i i i i i i i
n n n n n n n n n n n n n n n n n n n n n n n n n n n n n n
g g g g g g g g g g g g g g g g g g g g g g g g g g g g g g

silent buddha
stranded in waikiki
stands still
feels sad
for all the people
rushing by . . .

On the Beach

a poet
is a fisherman
of sorts

instead of fish
he brings home
poems

Everything Is Poetry to Me

well, who can

     say it's NOT

     poetry?

i hang out

       my dong

    and piss on

       a potted

          palm

CONVINCED!

Palolo

because everything
is poetry
      to me
I can write
"piss makes papayas
              sweet"
stumbling around Palolo

No One Understands The Sea—Upon Receipt Of My 33rd Rejection Notice

no one understands my poetry—

to understand my poetry
you got to understand my philosophy

no one understands my philosophy—

to understand my philosophy
you got to understand me

no one understands me—

to understand me
you got to understand Hawaii

no one understands Hawaii—

to understand Hawaii
you got to understand the Sea

no one understands the Sea

NO ONE UNDERSTANDS MY PHILOSOPHY!
NO ONE UNDERSTANDS THE SEA!
NO ONE UNDERSTANDS HAWAII!
NO ONE UNDERSTANDS ME!

rejection notices? here's thirty three!
NO ONE UNDERSTANDS MY POETRY!
NO ONE UNDERSTANDS THE SEA!

... an old black crab
            crawls down the long beach
            with nothing in its claws ...

... a wasted bee
            without a Sting
            drowns himself in the Sea ...

EGGS

EGGS

EGGS

EGGS

EGGS

EGGS

EGGS

EGGS

EGGS

EGGS

EGGS

EGGS

EGGS

EGGS

EGGS

EGGS

EGGS

```
H M I O
A Y S F
L F F F
F A A
  C L
  E L
  I N
    G
```

HALF MY FACE IS FALLING OFF

icarus in a corner
burning wings
black smoke clings
very bad
man i get so mad
cleaning mirrors

i eat meat!

out of compassion
for the stray cat
i órdered fish
instead of meat

but when i gave
some to the cat
he didn't want it
just stared back

'i want meat'

shit!
what a bummer
next time
i eat meat!

Jack Kerouac's Bones

he never
   made any money
  on his books
but lately
   i heard
  lotta people
     who never knew him
  make money
     on his bones.

Lost Weekend

two days gone
drunk on sake
suddenly find
myself home again
reading sutras

all the people
waiting in line
at the bank
each one's arms
folded across their chests

funny—huh?
back
    of the line
my arms
    behind my back.

when young
   he had a bad temper
now old
   he's got it
            no more

come on
           old man
get mad!

six days cloudy
didn't help—no
pale as a ghost
too much Cocteau

My Mistress

it's interesting
how girls moan
O GOD!
when they come

I think about it
alone by the sea

two white doves
fly from a
coconut tree
an old black crab
too old for anything
crawls down a
long black rock ...

I look up
gaze out at
the waves
keep coming

AH! MY MISTRESS
THE SEA!

satisfied
with a poem
aah!
i smile

One hundred haiku
and a neglected wife
unimpressed . . .

the coconut

the coconut
   on the beach
just sits there

A

'A

A'A

'A'A

A'A'A

'A'A'A'A

"A"

W. Westlake '79

120

Sunday Morning

i can understand it
i can understand it
i can understand it
i can't understand it.

two cents
in my pocket
and i'm thinking
of going to China—

RIDICULOUS

Punchbowl Crater

nothing to do i
      climbed up the side
of punchbowl

up top i looked
      down inside
the crater

gray ghosts danced
      in the black
black night

my legs
      my trousers
ripped to shreds

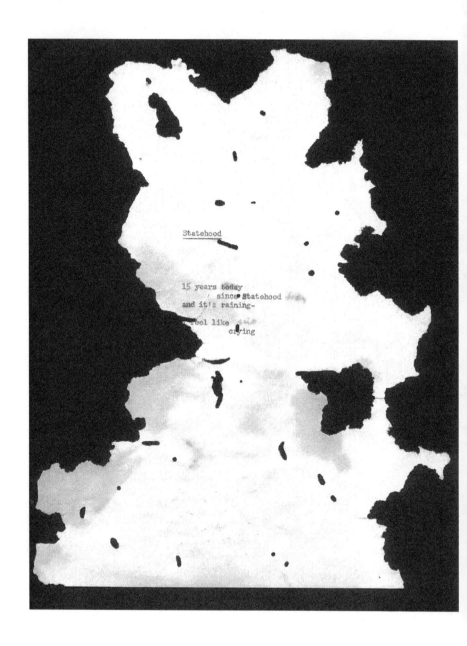

Statehood

15 years today
        since Statehood
and it's raining-

feel like
        crying

Statehood

15 years today
      since STATEHOOD
it's raining
i feel like
       crying . . .

i am a bread crumb

i am a bread crumb

i am a bread crumb on the kitchen
floor

there are ants
there are ants on the kitchen floor

i am a bread crumb
on the kitchen floor

there are ants
circling around me
like sharks,
wondering where to
begin . . .

i am an ant

i am an ant on the kitchen
floor

there is a bread crumb
there is a bread crumb on the kitchen floor

i am a hungry ant
there is a bread crumb

i think
i'll eat it
now . . .

i am no longer
a bread crumb

i am no longer
an ant

i am suddenly a man

i am suddenly a drowning
man

i am suddenly drowning
of thirst—

there is swirling water
all around me

Today's a Sad Day

the dog that usually
comes charging out
                    at me
            BARKING
today just sits there
looking sad

the other dog
        his playmate
that usually comes
charging and barking
                    too

yesterday was killed
by a car

i saw it all
            from the sidewalk

and it was sad

today is a sad day

for dogs
            and people,
                    too

After the Thunderstorm

pretty girls
            appear
            out of nowhere
each trailing
            after her
a different
            scent—

i follow barefeet
            thru warm
            dew grass

feeling like some
            kind of god—

    after the thunder
                    storm . . .

it's amazing!

even in dreams
            the skull
        leaks badly

drip
drip
drip
down my spine

like warm rain
            dripping down
        tall tree
                    trunks

HULI

"Huli"   W. Westlake '79

must be
mind
that moves—
just now
over there
saw the wind
blow
a boulder
over

don't stop
or the mosquitoes
will get you

in the mountains
by the sea
stretching for guavas
climbing for lichee

gotta keep moving
or the mosquitoes
will get you

breathing ginger
gazing at bamboo

misty
    morning
        moon
bright over
      waikiki
all the tourists
           sleep

only we
     can see.

jesus rap
    staring at the ground
look up
    the old lady
      crying.

If I Wore a Tie

"where you
          going to get
MONEY
          for gas?"
questions
from my brother.
he's married
'i don't know'

"rumor is
          you're getting
MARRIED"
absurdity
from his wife—
she doesn't know.

lost in a dream
should i scream?

IF I WORE A TIE
I'D DIE!

Greedy men love to gather Wealth
Just like owls love having children
But the children grow up and eat the Mothers
Too much Wealth comes back and kills you!
Scatter it and Happiness is born!
Gather it and Disaster leaps up
Have no Wealth—have no Troubles
Go flap your wings in the Sky!

—translated from Han Shan

Pigs eat dead man's meat.
Men eat dead pig's guts—
Pigs don't hate man's stink,
Men even say pigs smell sweet!
When pigs die, throw 'em in the river.
When men die, dig the earth and hide.
For the pigs and men that don't eat each other:
Ah! The Lotus blossoms in bubbling soup!

—translated from Han Shan

POEMS

FROM

DOWN ON THE SIDEWALK IN WAIKIKI

(1972 to 1973)

last year i spent working as a janitor
down on the sidewalk in waikiki—
experiences ran from everything to
everything. i wrote poems to keep from
going insane ... (1973)

Down On The Sidewalk In Waikiki

No need feel sorry
    for the crippled man
    down on the sidewalk
      —in Waikiki

There are a lot more crippled
    minds
        limping around,
    feel sorry for them!

Down On The Sidewalk

down on the sidewalk

in waikiki

feeling more than sad

i wonder, silent

to myself

why i don't go

STARK

RAVING

MAD!

Down On The Sidewalk (In Waikiki)

down on the sidewalk
in waikiki
I
   SEE
      EVERYTHING
passing me:

lost souls
girls with nice asses,
businessmen
        with dirty assholes
        and shiny suits,

bums   pimps   whores
freaks   junkies   gigolos
and burnt out Amerikans . . .

they're
straight   bent
slimy   clean
women under the
        spell of the MOON
children learning
        the GAME too soon

policemen   hippies
Kahunas (a few)
fat sick Amerikans
and speedy Japanese

studs   cunts
rich   poor

perverts   weirdos
beggars   fools
crazy-men
and old people
                about to DIE . . .

they're all there
i tell you,
            man
from my seat
down on the sidewalk
in waikiki
I SEE EVERYTHING:
this gigantic PIG
                PARADE
            staggering by . . .

and across the street
unnoticed,
an old Hawaiian
    slowly sweeps
  the sidewalk
                clean
            with a fallen
            coconut leaf:

away,
        you fools
    he whispers,
                away!

there was this strange smell
first thing in the morning
when the janitor, crazy fool
first opened the door:
shit? anger? despair?
what was it this time?
he wondered ...

the janitor suddenly wished
he'd brought some incense
to clean the air
of evil, of spirits, of evil

whatever the smell was
SOMETHING was WEIRD:
there was blood
all over the floor!

... and the Police
they found him
dead in the bathroom
and the janitor
spent all morning
cleaning blood
off the floor,
and glass ...

THE NAME OF THE GAME
IS PROFIT!
down on the sidewalk
in waikiki:
crazy guy all doped up
went right thru the
plateglass window
hungry, starving
for some BREAD

didn't find anything

BLEEDING
he went CRAZY
like a wounded animal
TRAPPED!
he lost his mind
went running
FRANTIC!
all over the store:

there was blood EVERYWHERE
on the floor
and high up
on the walls

the Name of the Game
is PROFIT all right
and when the janitor
(that's his job)
got down on his fucking knees
to clean up the mess
the smell of rotted
clotted
blood
ten times
just about made him
lose his GUTS!

HORRIBLE!
more than that:
HE JUST ABOUT
LOST HIS MIND!

in the bathroom
where they found him
bleeding
was the worst:
the floor was solid
blood—

the guy must have tried
to stop the bleeding
using two old
slimy sponges

no way

two slimy sponges
full, heavy
and much more
all over the floor—
gagging,
i flushed two blood-soaked
slimy sponges
down the toilet
away . . .

fingers sticky
from the blood
bleeding
from the glass
they gave the janitor
a ten dollar bill
for cleaning up
the mess

the janitor, i took it
out of my mind
and went straight to a place
    called HELL
                and spent it . . .

JANITOR—OKADAYA
WAIKIKI—HAWAII

cleaning piss
        off the floor
of the japanese
        tourist store

can't help thinking
        over and over

"these japanese
        businessmen
    are PIGS!"

A Savage Can't Live In Amerika

i always had this thing
about my hair:
it gets so long
it's FREAKY!
like a SAVAGE,
you know,
it's cool
you know, but

A SAVAGE
CAN'T LIVE
IN AMERIKA!

and Amerika
i tell you
is EVERYWHERE!

...and when you
run around NAKED
in the hot
HAWAIIAN SUN,
your skin
naturally
turns brown
DEEP DARK BROWN
like chocolate,
and hair
turns yellow like
GOLD!

gold hair
brown skin
half-naked
crazy grin
it's WEIRD
i know
i've seen my
self a SAVAGE
in plateglass
windows
down on the sidewalk
in waikiki

and sometimes
it SCARES ME
TO DEATH!

CRACKED

HUNKS
    of raw meat
down on the sidewalk
        in waikiki
look to me
like something
        OBSCENE!

but it's not
SO STRANGE
in waikiki
      where dirt's
    expensive
and bricks
     are cheaper
        than rocks—

can't stand
to look at it
any longer
i get up
and FLEE
the MONSTER

WAIKIKI!

washing windows
    dirty janitor sweats
clean tourist asks
    "how do you get . . ."
before he's finished
    tell him
        EAT SHIT!

THESE DROPS

down on the sidewalk
in waikiki
i wring my mind
like a blood-soaked sponge
and get
      these
      drops:

"the girls asses
      are nice
but the World's
      in bad shape
you can see it
in their
      Eyes—"

BURNT OUT!
WASTED!
WIPED OUT!

D For Disgusting

from my seat

down on the sidewalk

in waikiki

i watch Amerika

limp by—

FAT

AND

DISGUSTING!

OUT OF MIND

to give my poems

BITE

i sit all day

down on the

           sidewalk

in waikiki

watching the

        PIG PARADE

limp by . . .

i watch them

           the Pigs—

the Pigs,

        they watch me—

it's enough to drive

any man

        CRAZY

i write

i write

TOTALLY OUT OF

        MY MIND

CHRISTMAS DAY, 1972

washing windows

down on the sidewalk

in waikiki

tourists again

they're asking me

the way to

the Catholic Church—

since it's Christmas Day

i oblige them pointing gladly

pointing a finger

up my ass:

"GO STRAIGHT AS AN ARROW

TO HELL!"

CHRISTMAS DAY

Christmas day's
        a holiday
the janitor
        doesn't have
    to work!

so he sleeps
        and sleeps
has weird dreams
        and gets up late

outside
a fine rain
falling.

WHAT?
you never seen
a human
     being
    before?
well then what
   the fuck
       you staring
    for,
      ASSHOLE!

no shirt
no shoes
bald head
brown skin—
      taking a short
    cut
through Honolulu
      zoo
     people all look
       at me
      like i should
be in some
   kind
     of
    cage . . .

MUTANTS!
PIGS!

i just hang around
the lion cages:
    a lepered sparrow
   pecking on
       bloody
     bones

Blood Stains

down

    on the sidewalk

in waikiki

      i look

        like a Haole

but i'm not:

i got

    ROYAL HAWAIIAN BLOOD!

really!

    i got

but by now

     it's probably

        all gone:

seeing what's

     going on

i BLEED

a lot

and no way

     will

       that

         stop . . .

The Kahuna Of Waikiki

the bum Hawaiian
came up to me
down on the sidewalk
in waikiki
put out his hand
said he needed smokes
asked me for
some change

i reached in my pocket
looking for the cash
asked how he was doing

the World these days
so STRANGE—
    "gotta know where
    they are first
    before they know
    where you are"
he said, "I could
go home RIGHT NOW!"

paranoid looking around
wanting to leave
i gave my last dollar
to the Kahuna of Waikiki
mumbling INSANELY
stumbling down
the crowded street . . .

THE DIRTY OLD KAHUNA

the dirty old Kahuna
                              yawns
another morning
                              wakes up
from under his coconut
                              tree
the Kahuna stands up
brushing last night's
                              sand
off his back, his hair
                  his hands

the dirty old Kahuna
puts on a dirty old aloha
                              shirt

nothing to win
nothing to lose
the Kahuna goes stumbling
straight into
            the Heart of
                        Waikiki

on the sidewalk, ah!
this morning the Kahuna
                              finds
something special:
wilted but nice
                  he puts it on
ah, still smells good!
the dirty old Kahuna
                        SMILES!

friday the 13th
full moon tonight
wearing a beat-up
old orchid lei
that some dumb tourist
threw away
            the Kahuna stands
on the corner
Kalakaua and Kaiulani
calls over to his friend
                    come over
and asks him for
                some change
for cigarettes
            and something
                        to eat!

his friend, the janitor
of waikiki
empties
        his wallet
                GLADLY!
                WHY?
'cause down on the sidewalk
  in waikiki

NOTHING'S FREE!

PAID BY THE SEA

"PIGS! EAT SHIT!
HEY PIGS!"
i practice
by the sea
on my way down
to the sidewalk
in waikiki:
the Amerikan Legion
Parade . . .

i didn't think
i should write this
what if
maybe i get
caught—
in trouble
then what?
the Pigs
will read it
and nail me
right?

said fuck it
sat down
and wrote it . . .

guess it was
right and the
right thing
to do
first poem
i got paid for
paid by the sea:
two dollar bills
found
right there
on the beach—

one for the Kahuna
and one for me

waikiki
> with all its people
> is still
> > a lonely place

as rats climb
the coconut trees
> > the meat
keeps broiling and
> fat pigs still
> > slide out of
> cadillacs
> > OINKING
fingering the slimy
> green GOD
of waikiki:

"the whores don't
> want your cock, man
they want your
> MONEY!"

. . . as rats climb
the coconut trees
> > going insane
down on the sidewalk
> > in waikiki i
> remember the kahuna
how he treated
> pretty girls:
swatted them away
> like flies!

i stumble sad
> and lonely
down the crowded
> streets

. . . as rats climb
the coconut trees . . .

The Devil Of My Life

got an expensive
habit to
        maintain
you know,
something
          called Life

so i have to
go to
     work every day
down on the sidewalk
         in waikiki:

like a young punk monkey
facing a giant ape
every morning
i face off waikiki

and when i meet
that Joe Paradise
in the heart of
the concrete jungle
I'LL SPIT
IN HIS FACE!

giant monster
sick and evil
WAIKIKI
i never win
leave there
every morning
SCREAMING
        RUNNING
the Devil of my Life
       hungry again
snapping
     at my heels!

Lost

last night
in a dream
someone stapled
the sea
to my mind

it was my Badge:
i was invited
to a party!

all the lunatics
the sages
the madmen
of waikiki
were there

and the Kahuna
he was there
too, of course
the highest!
the happiest!
the guest of HONOR!
all the others
lifting beers
around him
drinking!
laughing!
singing ...

but that's
all gone now—
i woke up
lost
banished
down

on the sidewalk
in waikiki
looking
looking
can't see
THE KAHUNAS
ALL GONE!
tears sliding
down my cheeks
salting
my lips
my god!
what am i doing
where
am
   i?

Mutants Everyone

brown skin
gold hair
no shirt
            no shoes
some dumb
            ass
came up to me
down on the sidewalk
            in waikiki
asked if i
            dyed my hair?

IDIOT!
    i told him
YOU FOOL!

just can't look
like a human being
these days,
            can you?
people FREAK!

THEY ALL LOOK
LIKE MUTANTS
TO ME!

Golden Boy
meets Miss Clairol—
they fuck and maybe
something is born—

i don't know:

either you mutate

or you

DIE!

MANGO-JUICE SLOBBER

tourist lady
walked up to me
down on the sidewalk
in waikiki
didn't say a word
just stared

i stared back
couldn't believe it
how white—how smooth
her legs

she looked at me
like a wildman
eating a mango
in the sun

i just laughed
an INSANE laugh
and she ran away
fast
mango-juice slobber
drying on my face . . .

i sat there awhile
in a daze

the Parade
looking interesting

i walked on
picking my teeth

JESUS FREAKS

if i took jesus
in my heart
the Sun wouldn't
shine

and if the Sun
didn't shine
the Sun
God RA would
be angry!

i
WORSHIP
THE
SUN!

and make the Sun
not shine
is the
last thing in the world
i want
to do

so . . .
i told the
jesus freak
can't you see
i don't want
to stand here
down on the sidewalk
in waikiki
and PRAISE THE LORD!

he, the jesus freak
looked at me puzzled
head uplifted
ah! the Sun
warm on my face
as
i
walked
down
the
street . . .

The Hawaiian

down on the sidewalk

in waikiki

the old Hawaiian

      kept looking

      up in the sky

i wondered

      why?

what's he looking

      at?

looked up to see

mynah birds frolicking

      in coconut

         trees

of course!

of course!

wasted

full moon's gone
and left me

lost and sick
like a lost
sick
dog ...

dead dog
on the road

what's it mean?

should i SCREAM?

yesterday today
tomorrow
FOREVER all a
sad
sick
DREAM ...

if i wore
a tie
i'd DIE!

noose up tight
they got me
hanging
already

feet dangling
down on the sidewalk
in waikiki

as the world
goes
spinning
by ...

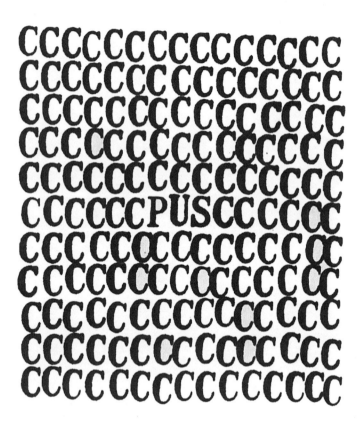

VITAMIN C HAS REDUCED THE PUS

Wish I

could empty

my Mind

like an

ashtray . . .

outside the hall of dreams

voice of raindrops

voice of leaves

like an earthquake
my mind
begins to tremble

frantic i scribble
another poem . . .

Haiku all night she hates me for it

Fleeting as mango season her love

Bird calls my only morning consolation

Ancient ruins only way to describe our love

She loves me she hates me which one tonight

Her name over and over in the wind

Starving to Death

Swallowing saliva
all the way
       to the bank
get there
       at the door—
too late
it's closed

paycheck in my hand
stomach groans
hunger got me
       by the balls

salting the wound

after the poetry reading
i find a poster with
my name on it—
i rip the poster
down!

"Poets of Today"
 new cat Yama
pissed on it!

studying the poets
lightning! thunder!
                    CRASH!
i slam the book!
decide right then
                    and there:
A POET MUST FIND
HIS OWN VOICE!

i listen for mine

NOTHING

what even makes one
            think he's
                    a poet
                anyway?

i wonder

three days rain
and i'm pale
            as a ghost!
"Let the poets
            play their
        GAMES
i'll just stay naked
        in bed
        all day

and listen to the rain!"

wrapped in white sheets
i listen

        even though
     my eyes are closed
i still can see
          the lightning
     FLASH!

listen

there is only ...
     voice of raindrops

     voice of leaves

Moving In <small>(THE UNCARVED BLOCK)</small>

arranging my room:
hang a painting here
move a desk there
then suddenly i remember
THE UNCARVED BLOCK!

left it down in the trunk
of my car outside
in the rain i walk
bare feet down moss wet
slippery steps.

ah! there's the moon
in a mud puddle
i look up, no shit
it's just a street light

i open the trunk
of my rusted out car
with a shiny golden key

THE UNCARVED BLOCK
sitting there
heavy
i lift it to my shoulder
carry it
like atlas
carrying the world
back up the never ending
moss wet slippery
steps
  will i make it?
finally in my room

i drop
THE UNCARVED BLOCK
heavy
like the cares of the world
off my back
onto the floor

released
now what?

sweating pouring
like streams
out of my head
from my forehead
on THE UNCARVED BLOCK
i put a squeaky
old fan, magic
wind maker
flip on the switch
lay back, ah! ooah!
and enjoy the BREEZE

LOLOLOLOLOLOLOLOLOLOLO
LOLOLOLOLOLOLOLOLOLOLO
LOLO LOLOLOLOLOLOLOLOLO
LOLOLOLOLOLOLOLOLOLOLO
LOLOLOLOLOLOLOLOLOLOLO
LOLO LOLOPAKALOLOLOLO
LOLOLOLOLOLOLOLOLOLOLO
LOLOLOLOLOLOLOLOLOLOLO
LOLOLOLOLOLOLOLOLOLOLO
LOLOLOLOLOLOLOLOLOLOLO
LOLOLOLOLOLOLOLOLOLOLO

Pakalolo

182

Two people

in bed

grinning about something

55 ways to get ahead

get a job
style your hair
wear shoes
eat meat voraciously
push
smoke cancer sticks
drink wine
get married
watch TV
shop at safeway
play the stocks
sell real estate
gobble speed
shine your shoes
eat at mcdonalds
become a poet
believe in greed
read the newspaper
get into politics
drive a porsche
grow a moustache
wear silkies
talk big
act rich
always smile
wear masks
step on people
give the hippie handshake
stab backs
don't care
write checks

take out loans
kiss ass
suck cock
sell your soul
smoke dope
dance in discotheques
look important
carry a briefcase
strut around
stay out of the sun
don't worry
use deodorant
brush with crest
shave daily
scrub your asshole with soap
cheat on your wife
live in a condominium
wear double-knit pants
tie your tie
don't think
be cool
talk bullshit
play games
love all lies!

Steaming Streets (poem found on a leaf)

sandy beach
like miami
       beach
honolulu like
        L.A.—
saturday's
       a weird day—
all the people
come out

        . . . rootless
     i drift
       aimless
  i stumble
      homeless
in my own
     home . . .

the sky is
     clouded
the comet
on its way
      i yawn in manoa
  valley rain
carrying my swim-fins
         around black
        steaming streets!

AMAZING!
found a pen
     on the street
all wet and
     it works!

i sit in wet grass
    and write this
  poem on a leaf

RECHARGE

first thing in the
            morning
        i wake up and
immediately hunt
                and kill
            fifty-seven
                    fleas!

TERRIBLE!

it's either God
        or me
i tell
    the fleas
    one at a time
popping them
                beneath my
                        thumb:
'namuamidabutsu'
                    crack!
'namuamidabutsu'
                pop!
it's either
        God or
                me
i tell each
        flea
            full of blood:
        my blood!

it begins to rain
i just lie there

                feeling like shit
        windows wide open
                                getting soaking wet

        the fleas
                hop
        i don't care:
                        'namuamidabutsu'
                        'namuamidabutsu'
                flea bites itching
        all
            over
                me
                        'namuamidabutsu'
                        'namuamidabutsu'
        i pray for
                my
                        self . . .

Native-Hawaiian

how we spose
feel Hawaiian anymoa
barefeet buying smokes
in da seven
eleven stoa . . . ?

The Tourist

the tourist
walks
makai—
straight
towards the mountains

Pua‘a

lahaina
is a town
of pigs—
and I don't mean
pua‘a!

Breadfruit

breadfruit
what's that?
the tourist gasped—
should'a stuffed one
in her face!

A Hawaiian Boy Speaks Out of Place

You never learned her old recipes
You never learned her sewing patterns
You never learned her language
You never learned her culture
You never learned her religion

So how come you walk so far ahead
of your Japanese grandmother
like your grandfather did?

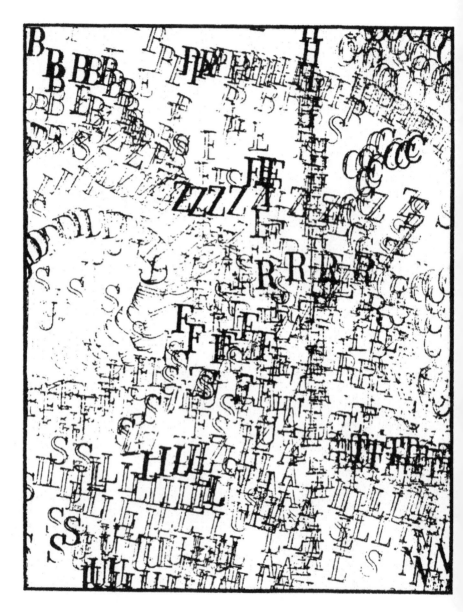

Broken English

CONSTRUCTION

"everything that's happened
has happened before
and is happening right now and will
happen again?"

drunk
i rub my blood-shot
eyes seeing weird
designs

my room has no curtains
my shoulders are
cold:
eyes closed i wonder
what windows
are for ...

"there is no space
no time: everything's
too wide: infinity's
in a square inch: the universe
stretches
endlessly"

i stand up naked
in this vast and
meaningless universe
(the neighbors can't see)
i close each window
slowly: the night
sky
filled with stars!

i lay back down:
the absurdity of it all:
tomorrow i go fill
in a lake ...

late to work
i brush my teeth
with my hard
hat
on

either my head's
            swelled up
or my hard hat's
                shrunk
every morning
i leave the house
thinking i forgot
            something
what—
my
    self?

one thing the foreman
doesn't like me
picking up
seashells i
uncovered in the
muck

i hear him yelling
at me from above
i just lean on my
shovel
examining an ancient
shell

too tired
   to write
      anything
after work
   i whistle
      my poems

That Smell

i get up
sit down
get up—

can't escape it:
that smell

all day
down in the sewers
of the world of life
i just can't
escape it:

that smell

lord knows i tried:
soap, shampoo,
deodorant, cologne
still

that smell

i keep hearing
knocks
on the door:

i get up
sit down
get up

can't escape it:
that smell
         of shit!

rain-out
    at work
        today
i open my lunch
    pail on
        the beach

finger nails

down in the sewer
all day
fired after only
9 days
i clean my fingernails
one last time

beer cans
  on the beach
    acting like crabs!

my life's twilight
a bell sounds
    i enjoy
        the evening cool.

White House Jabberwocky

Congress	issue	small
leery	personal	substantial
more	Dept.	history
less	U.S.	concern
demand	agree	applause
atmosphere	discussions	pushed
proceed	Pres.	culture
tense	top	public
sensitive	defense	qualified
diplomacy	phase	available
claims	out	community
commission	live	funds
create	use	no
reparations	explosives	lack
joint	Island	merit
succeed	archaeologists	essential
exception	public	positive
accused	open	Image
stand	research	Hawaiian
failing	plans	development
Hawaiians	parts	youngsters

GOD

God is a fat turd floating
God is a steaming bowl of rice
God is a toothache aching
God is a lie . . .

God is a runny nose
God is a tasty lip
God is a swollen vagina
God is a conch shell . . .

God is a limp cock hanging in the wind
God is a pen out of ink
God is a giant tit
God is a voyeur watching shadows bounce . . .

God is a wadded kleenex
God is a pubic hair curled on the kitchen floor
God is a pile of shit steaming in the moonlight
God is a purple haze . . .

God is a bulldozer dozing
God is a squirming electric eel shocking
God is a bowtie
God is a rusty nail . . .

God is a giant cockroach
God is a starry night
God is a slimy toad
God is a rocky mountain bear . . .

God is rotten watermelon
God is ripe papaya
God is a pineapple
God is a sweetsour shrimp . . .

God is black mud foaming
God is a threefoot earthworm
God is an octopus tangling
God is a hard hat . . .

God is an empty beer bottle
God is a teeshirt full of pukas
God is a chocolate milkshake
God is a cigarette butt . . .

God is a hand without fingers
God is a toilet bowl flushing
God is peanut butter
God is a swamp . . .

God is a typewriter that sticks
God is a stop-watch
God is a sinking ship
God is a horny fucker . . .

God is out-of-space
God is out-of-time
God is an ashtray
God is a dirty sock . . .

God is a filthy pair of panties
God is a salt sea breeze
God is an open window
God is a bad dream . . .

God is a lubricated rubber
God is a razor's edge
God is a cup of too sweet coffee
God is an LSD flashback . . .

God is a TV set
God is a wilted hibiscus
God is J. Edgar Hoover
God is Absurd . . .

God is a mental reject
God is a construction worker with holes in his boots
God is seaweed glowing
God is a thrashing shark . . .

God is a monkey swinging
God is nervous
God is trembling
God is a bat hanging upside down . . .

God is made in Japan
God is a silk aloha shirt
God is a salty peanut
God is an iced-cold beer . . .

God is a dumptruck covered with mud
God is a yellow volkswagen
God is a banshee screaming
God is a female in heat . . .

God is a chopstick chopping
God is a mirror burning bright
God is tired
God is a sleeper in the nude . . .

God is a telescope
God is a fighter pilot
God is an oriental
God is a vietnam veteran . . .

God is epileptic
God is retarded
God is a blownout candle
God is Bridget Bardot . . .

God is Mishima without his head
God is a nigger
God is a dirty beggar's bag
God is a toe lost in the Himalayan snow . . .

God is a crystal
God is a hospital
God is a Chinese cigarette
God is a broken neck . . .

God is a mango
God is a natural disaster
God is an intestine full of poisonous gas
God is simply ridiculous . . .

God is a sky-blue eye
God is a rotten egg
God is inside out
God is a blood-soaked sponge . . .

God is a pus-dripping abscess
God is a cancerous anus
God is a chain smoker
God is a lost soul . . .

God is an old hag
God is a clit
God is pregnant
God is a hangman's noose . . .

God is blind
God is deaf
God is dumb
God is always spaced-out ...

God is a hunchback
God is a hemorrhoid
God is a pimple on a cock
God is a white cloud billowing ...

God is a buffalo rumbling through the bush
God is a millionaire model speeding in her porsche
God is a fat man twiddling his thumbs
God is a poet about to crack ...

God is a hollow egg-shell
God is a burnt-out crab
God is a black stone
God is a dead cat on the road ...

God is an elephant rambling
God is a mosquito stinging
God is incense swirling
God is sleepy ...

God is a dark sky full of rain
God is a cargoship full of nothing
God is a sunburned face
God is a lazy oaf ...

God is a baby crying
God is a polio shot
God is an iron lung
God is a custard pie ...

God is a woman moaning in the night
God is a hypodermic needle
God is an abandoned car
God is a staggering vagabond bum . . .

God is a 12-inch cock
God is a scrambled brain
God is a single sand grain
God is a blood-clot in the mind . . .

God is a stewed strawberry
God is a rope full of knots
God is a longhaired, bearded, dope-smoking hippie
God is a palm tree blowing in the wind . . .

God is an owl
God is an ox
God is a porcupine
God is tall grass bending . . .

God is a cold mountain stream
God is a refreshing spring breeze refreshing
God is a slimy lizard
God is skintight pants . . .

God is a gas pain
God is a smelly cunt
God is a young girl's ass, spread open
God is a blood-stained sheet . . .

God is a skin diver diving for life
God is a bleeding heart
God is a sweating foot
God is a discarded Tampax by the roadside . . .

God is a hairbrush full of dandruff
God is a finger up an asshole
God is a tough toilet tissue
God is a broken leg ...

God is fresh sashimi
God is cone sushi
God is a half-smoked joint
God is a map, crumpled, thrown away ...

God is a seemoi seed
God is a Communist
God is a dead battery
God is a pickled plum ...

God is a midget wrestler
God is a plastic Jesus
God is a rusty beer can on the beach
God is an itchy flea bite ...

God is a dancer's leg
God is a mud puddle
God is a mirage
God is a coconut washed up on shore ...

God is a clock that's stopped
God is a light bulb burnt out
God is a tatami mat
God is a bamboo walking stick ...

God is an exhausted mind
God is a spare tire
God is a telephone book
God is a phoney ...

God is a prison cell
God is a firing squad
God is an electric chair
God is a stiff neck ...

God is a full moon
God is a werewolf
God is a vampire
God is a naked sunbather ...

God is a plugged toilet
God is chicken shit
God is a vienna sausage stuck to the pot
God is a tear-soaked pillow ...

God is Adolf Hitler
God is Dead ...

God is carrot juice
God is a garbage pail
God is a giant whale
God is a dirty toenail ...

God is hot jasmine tea
God is sitar music
God is a lady to kiss
God is a cigarette after work ...

God is warm monkey brains
God is a Gahan Wilson cartoon
God is a sad, sick joke
God is only human ...

God is a carton of milk
God is a shadow
God is a child being born
God is destined to fail . . .

God is a gardenia blooming
God is a muscle freak flexing
God is a sideshow
God is Lawrence Welk . . .

God is a pink smoke bomb in your eye
God is an ice cube
God is rain in the afternoon
God is a 16-foot marijuana plant . . .

God is a police helicopter
God is a fresh pound of hashish
God is a madman eating lichee in the sun
God is an imbecile . . .

God is a papaya seed
God is a jelly bean
God is an avocado
God is a slithering snake . . .

God is the last match that went out
God is a cold six-pack
God is an underworld hitman
God is pissed . . .

God is a migraine headache
God is a screaming asshole
God is a bouncing bedspring
God is a three-legged giraffe . . .

God is a timid gambler
God is a paranoid personality
God is an impotent truck driver
God is a raving sex maniac . . .

God is brown rice
God is a weightlifter in the sun
God is mud splattering
God is insane . . .

God is a sopping underarm
God is a gliding bird resting its wings
God is a prickly cactus
God is a hairy crotch . . .

God is a saké jug
God is a shaved head
God is a juicy fart
God is a buttered bunghole . . .

God is a mongoose
God is a haupia cake
God is tooth decay
God is dog spelled backwards . . .

God is a hoax
God is a used car salesman
God is an airline stewardess
God is fucked . . .

God is a whirling dervish
God is a glue-sniffing teenager
God is a forty-foot wave
God is a mucus membrane . . .

God is a green light—go
God is a red light—stop
God is a mutant
God is a robot . . .

God is a thick spit
God is a traffic cop
God is a convicted felon
God is a grubby rodent . . .

God is a broken bootlace
God is a cannibal
God is Charles Bukowski's face
God is a baboon in disguise . . .

God is a mating dragonfly
God is a bright red ant
God is a lemon drop
God is an over-turned potato bug . . .

God is Whistler's mother
God is a limping sage
God is yesterday's onion
God is frothing at the mouth . . .

God is a fist in the face
God is a baby drowning
God is green piss
God is disgusting . . .

God is feverish
God is fatal
God is futile
God is a goddamn idiot . . .

God is a snoring caterpillar
God is an aborted fetus
God is an atom bomb
God is hot sperm sliding down a sleeping leg . . .

God is an opium eater
God is fermented bean-curd
God is moldy cheese
God is a sick dog howling at the moon . . .

God is bubble gum on the sidewalk
God is Babe Ruth striking out
God is a crippled man praying to God
God is a better day . . .

God is a purple glove
God is a purring cat
God is a greasy french fry
God is a black panther with glowing green eyes . . .

God is a tortoise creeping
God is a giant squid
God is a hairy spider
God is a man waking up with a vodka hangover . . .

God is a Republican
God is a machine gun
God is Harry Houdini stuck in a strait jacket
God is Jimmy Dean burning in a car crash . . .

God is Neal Cassidy speeding on
God is Jack Kerouac drinking beer
God is chains and shackles jingling
God is a junkie nodding out . . .

God is a sand crab peeking out of its hole
God is mayonnaise
God is Ronald McDonald
God is a rotten banana . . .

God is a sea-bird lost from the flock
God is Fyodor Dostoyevsky freezing in Siberia
God is Mao Tse Tung sleeping in a cave
God is Richard Nixon burning in Hell . . .

God is a gorilla eating grass
God is a chest lifted to the wind
God is a tubercular lung
God is Albert Einstein without underwear . . .

God is a bulging bicep
God is a sagging beer-belly
God is a spaceship
God is a puka-shell necklace on a man that can't swim . . .

God is a whistler in the dark
God is one of Celine's three dots
God is Takuboku's poems to eat
God is Hagiwara's squished toad . . .

God is Issa giving up
God is a tiger eating a deer
God is an idiot's ear glued to a transistor radio
God is amusing . . .

God is a paycheck over two hundred dollars
God is clutching emptiness like a breast
God is a tall weed someone let grow
God is a poet drinking lakes of saké . . .

God is a Halloween mask
God is kid's stuff
God is a poem that needs revising
God is a single blade of grass . . .

God is a black stone split open
God is a black dog
God is a pale face in a mirror
God is a ghost . . .

God is a boxer out for the count
God is a mosquito smashed
God is a cat fight in the middle of the night
God is a woman to wake up to . . .

God is a lover of lepers
God is a stone cold pillow
God is an apparition in the night
God is a maggot infested carcass . . .

God is a one-inch waterfall
God is a Hershey kiss
God is a $10000 dental bill
God is a plate piled high with pancakes . . .

God is a fly trapped on fly paper
God is a black black poem
God is a dreamer walking in his sleep
God is an eater, stuffed, about to pass out . . .

God is a hamburger steak, gravy on the rice
God is a shave-ice in the scorching summer heat
God is a madman muddling in his mind
God is $5.88 an hour . . .

God is a waste of paper
God is a lost soul searching frantically for a body
God is a fly praying to become a man
God is a bull bellowing at the moon ...

God
is
not
there ...

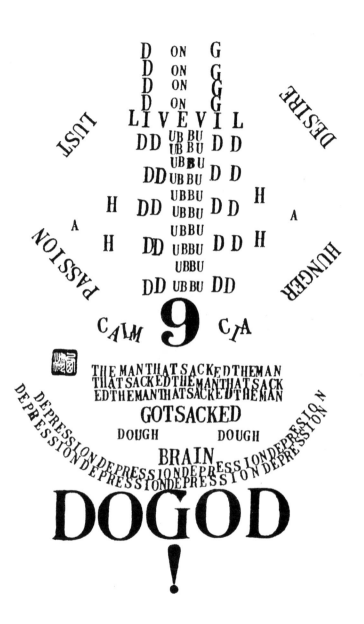

Dogo

THE QUESTION ARISES AS TO WHAT HE'S DOING?

S<small>PIT</small>

TOPA GRAP HER
TYOG RAP HER
TYPO GRAF HER

POEMS ARE MADE FROM
WORSD NOT IDEAS

BIBIBABA
BIBI BABA
BIBIBABA

POEMS ARE MADE FROM
IDEAS NOT WORDS

JESUS
SAVE
S

ECNALG   ENOG

MOSES   INVESTS

THANK YOU
FOR
NOT FARTING

WAYNE WESTLAKE

CONCRETE POETRY
AND
THE CHINESE WRITTEN CHARACTER

Typographical devices, employed with great daring, have given rise to a visual lyricism almost unknown before our time. These devices are capable of being carried much further, to the point of bringing about the synthesis of the arts — music, painting and literature. All this is merely a search for new, perfectly legitimate forms of expression."

—Guillaume Apollinaire
"The New Spirit and the Poets" (1917)

Some English concrete theoreticians have postulated the theory that single Chinese characters, by themselves, cannot stand concretely.

To insist that the human hand must exert some sort of influence on the word, an artistic manipulation so to speak, a "doing something to it," before it can truly be called concrete is certainly true for concrete poems written in the English language. But to insist that the same holds true for Chinese, a language of pictures, displays an ugly ignorance of the Chinese written language.

Since concrete poetry is the art of making visually stimulating pictures out of words, Chinese characters, single or otherwise, are concrete automatically, because every word in the Chinese language is already a visually stimulating pictograph. And a language of pictographs is one giant step ahead of a language of letters in the field of concrete poetry.

Single Chinese characters CAN and DO stand alone as concrete poems; especially the ancient images, where nowhere does the old Chinese saying ring more true: "One picture is worth ten-thousand words."

WAYNE WESTLAKE

MANIFESTO

Stab a book, any book. The letter you hit will be D.
Stab a book, any book. The letter you hit will be A.
Stab a book, any book. The letter you hit will be D.
Stab a book, any book. The letter you hit will be A.

Some computers have parts tinier than your fingernail. With five billion
circuits circling through them. Supposed to demonstrate intelligence.

It's lethal, yes. But the human hand is deadlier.

Nothing circles nothing. Hawaiians eat fish, fish eat Hawaiians.
Water a cow drinks turns to milk; water a snake drinks turns to venom.
Language the missionaries taught us was broken glass.
Our tongues are still bleeding.

As much as a beer belly deserves its place on a Hawaiian,
poetry deserves the death it gets!

If a banana can be a poem, anything can. Including your face, alphabet head!

If it wasn't for toads if it wasn't for termites
there would be no such thing.
If it wasn't for TV sets if it wasn't for aspirin
If it wasn't for airplanes cigarette butts cock
roaches gasoline and beer
there would be no such thing.

"like your hopes: nothing.
like your paradise: nothing.
like your idols: nothing.
like your politicians: nothing.
like your heroes: nothing.
like your artists: nothing.
like your gods: nothing."

GOD IS DEAD. KAMEHAMEHA IS DEAD. CHAIRMAN MAO IS
DEAD. DADA IS DEDA.

Cry.
Guts are spilling out
cement poems!

The eye sees. The brain doesn't.
The brain boggles. The eye doesn't.

If there was no grief
no hopelessness
no agony
no desperation
no doom
there would be
NOTHING

but blank pages.

If it wasn't for anarchy, if it wasn't for manic depression, if it wasn't for
chronic insomnia

there would be no such thing as

CONCRETE
POETRY

Think concrete. Think cement.
"concrete"
"cement"
What you see is what is meant.
Nothing more, nothing less.
Take it or leave it.

"Literature is in constant need of rebarbarization"

Unconsciousness drowns Consciousness

    卌 卌 卌 卌

    卌 卌 卌 卌

    卌 卌 卌 卌

    卌 卌 卌 卌

    卌 卌 卌 卌

Millionaires will lose millions
"Revolution is no dinner party"

but necessary for the barbarizing that must proceed

Like a ton of bricks thrown at you by a sweat-crazed mason,
not a mouthful of mushy peas spit in your face by a spoiled brat,
a concrete poem
should bust your head open!
Attack your brains like famine-frenzied sharks devouring every last crumb of

LOGIC AND REASON AND RATIONALITY

Kiss the lyrical poets, bite off and spit out their tongues!
Hug the intellectual poets, twist and snap off their heads!
Fondle the technical poets, lick and suck out their eyeballs!

MENTAL BRUTALITY!

Got enough TNT? Enough grenades? Try blow up a concrete poet:

Like blowing up air!

227

On Having an Intelligent Conversation with My Dog

If you didn't have pointed ears
would the wind howl?

If you didn't have a wet nose
would your dog shit stink?

If you didn't have a floppy tongue
would the tall grass taste sweet?

If you didn't have luau feet
would the lava be hot?
                  ful

If you didn't have bulging eyes
would the sunset streak?

Dog
tell me
how does Dan Inouye
clap?

LITERATURE IS IN NEED OF BARBARIZATION

My Dog Is Panting

Deep in ohia forest
I heard an engine start up
so I sat my dog down
in tall wet grass
and gave him a choice
of sticks
a light one and a heavy one
he took the heavy one
like a bird of prey clenched
firmly between his teeth

And all the dogs started barking
and all the roosters started crowing
and it was dawn

The cows in the pasture below
are causing a ruckus of moos (this morning)
I've hiked my cigarettes
all the way up this mountain
for a still moment just like this
only to find I brought a lighter
that's out of gas

Now what would a commando guerrilla
in Nicaragua do?
sit on a rotten hāpuʻu stump
sucking on an unlit cigarette
hiding from the Green Harvest
helicopter?

My dog is panting
try again that gutless lighter
no dice—move out!

Never
never walk down an open road
I heard that in the army
and careful not to put a single boot
print in the mud even though
my stomach's growling and
I haven't eaten meat in
three weeks

Every once and a while
I still have to stop
deep in the forest
and ask myself
where are we?

Sending My Dog to College

As my boy goes charging
through the thick torch ginger
and returns to me panting
and covered with dew

I wonder
if I chop enough stalks
could I send my dog
to college?

Then I remember my starving family
and think of how much mochi
crunch it would take
to feed them
my boy can dig and sleep in the dirt
but how 'bout my wife and daughter?

After over a third of a century
I've finally found my forte
chopping ginger stalks
maybe someday my boy will graduate
PhD in catching bees!

Every night
I lie down
and the fleas eat dinner . . .

"Can't

be a hermit yet"

he said,

the young fool

One inch long
        like Buddha's

Kawabata's penis

after the poetry reading

               for W. S. Merwin

Shaking hands

    with "The Poet"

I held my tongue . . .

TEACHING MY DOG BUDDHISM
WELCOME
FROM THE NEW FRONTIER WHERE
QUARKS & QUASARS, NEUTRINOS
ELNINOS & COMPUTER CHIPS
RULE OVER THE UNSEEN HANDS
THAT PUPPET OUR ACTIONS. HAPPY
NEW YEAR FROM THE NEW FRONTIER
REMEMBER WHAT THE CHINESE
SCHOLAR SAID.
    "WE'VE GONE TOO FAR TO
PULL
BACK ON THE REINS."
OR AS THE CHAIRMAN SAID. TO
"PROGRESS IN THE WRONG DIRECTION
IS NOT PROGRESS AT ALL."
AND FINALLY THERE IS THAT
    VIETNAMESE PROVERB.
  "THE TREE WANT TO STAND
STILL BUT THE WIND WON'T
   LET IT."

TEACHING MY DOG BUDDHISM

Must be going crazy—

my favorite poet lately

has been me!

East and West

East

I'm afraid

does not

meet West—

they collide!

hey man—look

      the cherry blossoms

how quick they bloom

how quick they fall

just like you

KAIULANI

Must be

the Hawaiian blood—

that rainbow

recalls a

woman . . .

Afterword: The Poems

Wayne Edward Kaumualii Miller Westlake apparently destroyed all of his high school writing and probably most of his work produced while he was a student at the University of Oregon (1966 to circa 1969).[1] That said, Westlake also left hundreds of poems in various states of completion and organization, and this raised problems about how to choose and arrange his work. Long before his death, he had organized his unpublished poetry into various packets and files, some carefully typed and delicately hand-bound. Many of his manuscripts, poems, and drafts were chronologically arranged and gathered into several dozen envelopes and folders. He also retained hundreds of drafts of other poems that were hastily scribbled and randomly organized at best. He revised some of his poems multiple times; others remained unedited, and gems were scattered amid scores of scribbled poems, some illegible.[2] The best guidance about what to include from his archive came from one of Westlake's closest friends and a confidant over the years, Bo Hunter, who advised, "Be true to Westlake."

Among the questions that complicated the selection process was West-lake's own mixed attitude toward his publications. On the one hand, he was uncomfortable about publishing certain works until his parents, Frank Raymond and Elsa Marjorie Westlake, had passed away.[3] With hindsight, one can see why: his most gut-wrenching, satirical, and polemical pieces will no doubt be interpreted by some as irreverent, even blasphemous. On the other hand, he submitted and published scores of poems but left no record of his unpublished submissions. Lingering questions remain un-answered. For example, how many and which poems from his large body of unpublished work were rejected by editors and publishers from Hawai'i and elsewhere?[4] Did Westlake ever submit a substantive collection of work to larger publishing houses such as the University of Hawai'i Press, or to literary presses that he admired, such as City Lights Books or Black Spar-row Press? What befell certain poems that he read publicly in 1981, such as "Send Him a Pineapple or Two," a scathing reckoning with U.S. Senator Daniel K. Inouye and "My Suitcase Full of Teeth," which was critical of certain professors at the University of Hawai'i?[5]

This collection begins with one of Westlake's first published poems, a translation, "A Joke—To Tu Fu, After Li Po," which appeared in the *Chicago Review* in 1975, a gentle parody with a long reach:

On top Puff-Rice Mountain I meet Tu Fu!
Wearing a bamboo rain-hat in the noonday sun!
I ask, since parting, how come so thin?
Suffering from poetry, again?

The original poem, titled "About Tu Fu," was composed by 8th-century T'ang dynasty poet Li Po. Westlake's translation reaches back over 1,200 years to a friendship that flowered through poetry and wine drinking between the elder Taoist Li Po—risqué, flamboyant, and renowned—and a younger Confucian poet, the popular but more conservative Tu Fu. This translation, with its mischievous title and the rephrasing of the last two lines into questions instead of statements, is simultaneously lighthearted and serious. In a sense, Westlake himself becomes Li Po speaking to Tu Fu about poetry. "A joke," perhaps, but for Westlake as author and translator, crafting poetry was no joke, and imagining Tu Fu agonizing over his verses was something Westlake deeply empathized with, both humbly and playfully.[6] Finally, vivid interpretations within the translation ("On top Puff-Rice Mountain" and "Wearing a bamboo rain-hat in the noonday sun") reflect Westlake's careful reading of the original Chinese ideograms. His translations are flavorful and metrically unique, and one would be hard-pressed to find a better English rendition of this poem.[7]

The earliest poems in *Westlake* were composed in Oregon shortly before or after he dropped out of college. However, this collection has not been compiled in strictly chronological order; instead, the sequencing of poems observes a sense of movement, consciousness, and place that befits various periods in Westlake's life and work. Many of his early poems in this collection reveal reflections on self-identity and a poetic discipline aligned with his Ch'an Buddhist and Taoist studies, his lifestyle and practices. Care was given to provide as much open page space as possible, especially for Westlake's shortest poems. Two examples from a particular sheaf of typescript poems that barely escaped the ravages of termites are also included as illustrations—found art as concrete poetry—their near destruction made into representative art forms by hungry insects. Termites, probably disliking the taste of ink, nibbled through this one manuscript of short poems, but mostly avoided eating his typed words![8]

When Westlake left for Oregon in 1966, Honolulu was a sprawling city being preyed upon by ubiquitous construction cranes and undergoing relentless urbanization. In contrast, the Pacific Northwest's vast forests, streams, rivers, and lakes must have reminded him of the rural Maui of his early childhood and resonated with his growing passion for the paintings and calligraphy of Asian artists like the 13th-century Chinese painters Liang K'ai and Mu Ch'i and their latter-day disciples, the 16th- and 17th-century Japanese artist-poet-abbots Takuan and Hakuin. Part of what drew him to these works was the spare use of ink and brushwork along with a blending of calligraphy and poetry into the paintings themselves, seemingly ordinary images rendered with time-honored wit and unpretentious spontaneity.[9] These and the imagistic, concrete qualities of both the ancient and modern Chinese ideogram would influence his aesthetic for a lifetime.

Westlake studied the art of the short poem, which he wrote and refined throughout his career. His craftsmanship in this genre rests in the subtraction or reduction of information, with a light yet firm touch, absences within his poems expanding and enlarging the meaning of his work. In poems like "the naked child / pats the stream rocks / 'hee—hee—hee!'" he characteristically layers perspectives: the literally naked, tittering toddler patting the stream rocks; a flashback to the poet's own youth and innocence; an indigenous connectedness and consciousness that regards rocks as living entities, sacred and animate; onomatopoeia evoking the sounds from both the child and the stream, rendered in the line 'hee—hee—hee!'; momentary enlightenment or epiphany captured in a simple scene; multiple allusions to poems with naturalistic settings juxtaposing laughter with or poking fun at human fallibility; and finally, a playful notion that this scene may be entirely illusory, evoked purely from his or the child's imagination.[10] Like the epigrams of Greece and Rome, the ubiquitous short-poem form of Africa, the Americas, Asia, and the Middle East, and the poetic sayings from the oral traditions of Oceania, Westlake's own short poems invite recitation and reflection—each rippling with allusions to poets and their works before him.

Westlake's earliest unpublished poems, over 120 of them in typescript, at times depict humans as no more significant than, say, a cat or a squirrel.

One includes a Ch'an style, brush-and-ink painting of a crescent moon collocated with a typescript poem:

> silent
> still—
> the moon

These early poems are by turns calm, contemplative, and serene, often playful, celebratory records of humans intersecting, sometimes merely fleeting interstices, with images of rain, moonlight, sunshine, seasons, trees, mountains, and nature's smaller creatures, bugs, frogs, turtles, ducks, along with plants, blades of grass, and dandelions:

> Spring:
> The weeds in bloom—
> O I'm happy!

Westlake's sense of joy as expressed in the poem above relates not only to the new season but exalts the humble and the spurned, not unlike himself. Spring is not discriminating, and the disdained weeds, too, are blossoming. The poem is also an homage to haiku poets and is reminiscent of Santōka (1882–1940), who wrote: "Those who do not know the meaning of weeds do not know the mind of Nature. Weeds grasp their own essence and express its truth."[11] Westlake's happiness is transient, for spring passes, the weeds are either cut down or they die in winter; nevertheless, the poet celebrates this moment unabashedly.[12]

These early poems mark a tribute, particularly, to the imagery of naturalist haiku poet Issa. One is also reminded of 'ōlelo no'eau, short "poetic proverbs" integral to Hawaiian orature and a specific genre of an indigenous literary tradition that relies heavily on brevity with subtle imagery and wide-ranging allusion as well as word play and instruction.[13] Westlake's reverence for nā pōhaku, the sacred stones of his native lands, emerge in yet another short poem:

> Looks of disbelief:
> I'm on my knees
> Washing a rock.

Is the narrator of this poem a child or an adult? The line "Looks of disbelief" suggests the latter, contrasting with Westlake's earlier poem about the naked, laughing child patting rocks in a stream. Here, the poet displaces biblical allusions—disbelieving passersby, humble genuflection, washing of an honored guest's feet—with imagery associated with idolatry; the poet endures expressions of reluctance and discomfort while on both knees, cleansing, as if ritually, a sacred stone. This poem reverberates with allusions to "Kaulana nā Pua," the melodious Hawaiian song that to this day defies the 1893 overthrow of the Hawaiian monarchy by American politicians, businessmen, and descendants of missionaries. Westlake's short poem employs, albeit subtly, images of similar resistance.[14] Much later, in 1980, Westlake wrote: "Cultural, political, socio-economic and religious bias might plague our [Hawaiian] race and we might not be able to agree on much. But on one thing we certainly agree: All land is sacred. It was given to us by the gods and no man can take it away."[15]

Yet another poem contrasts the significance of nā pōhaku:

Ancient Stone

the girl i've
been staying with
starts her Cadillac.

i wait
in the shade
examining an ancient stone.

The world of the "girl," her Cadillac, and her poet lover (or friend) is carefully underplayed. However, long after the relationship between the two is over, long after the Cadillac is towed to the scrap yard, and far beyond the life of the poet himself, the ancient stones of Hawaiʻi will remain, sacred and steadfast: "I ka ʻai kamahaʻo o ka ʻāina, the astonishing food of the land."[16] Westlake's unpublished manuscripts from this period of his life document a time of respite and reflection amidst abandon, as in the poem "Brittle Bones": "sixty six / to seventy two / man, it burned / me out / how 'bout you." Westlake's poem above contrasts sharply with his persona of the "enlightened" poet writing of solitude and nature. Instead, this piece documents a lifestyle from 1966 to 1972 that combined a variety of activities: "eh—you / don't give me / any of your / acid enlightenment." By 1972, he was back in Hawai'i for good, his native lands now rumbling with discontent amidst rampant overdevelopment and the growing domination of a Hawai'i obsessed if not controlled by American culture, tourism, and corporate U.S. military interests.

Particularly dramatic and singular is a collection of thematically linked poems located past the midway point in Westlake's work, titled "Down on the Sidewalk in Waikiki." Never published, he composed this unique collection from 1972 through 1973 while working as a janitor at "Okadaya," a store located in the heart of Waikīkī.[17] Typescript and attractively hand-bound, the poems are crafted with energy and rendered with an acerbic tone—outraged, hurt, and alienated. Westlake blasts away at Waikīkī's rampant tourism and American materialism, crafting the polemical into art with a razor's edge.[18] These poems are filled with Westlake's teachings and critiques that echo ancestral and poetic traditions, be they Asian, Polynesian, or western. Like poets Han Shan and Catullus, Hawaiian authors David Malo and Samuel Mānaiakalani Kamakau, Tongan satirist Epeli Hau'ofa and Samoan novelist and poet Albert Wendt, Westlake was no social equivocator. His critiques of tourist culture and the tyranny of the American majority are interwoven with seething depictions of his ancestral home as a place irrevocably changed. Waikīkī becomes symbol and metaphor for the colonization of his own mind, of his native world as Kanaka Maoli—native Hawaiian—and of his indigenous nation, language, history, and culture. This posthumously published series of poems uniquely reflects not only the political ferment of the Civil Rights and anti–Vietnam War movements of the late 1960s and early 1970s, but most significantly foreshadows modern Hawaiian resistance movements. Ironically, unknown to Westlake at the time when he originally composed "Down on the Sidewalk in Waikiki," vigorous literary activism by politically outspoken indigenous authors and artists in Oceania had also emerged, particularly in Papua New Guinea (independent in 1975).[19]

Westlake's perceptions of social and cultural inequities were heightened while he worked as a janitor in Waikīkī. About 25 years old at the time, and determined to earn his bachelor of arts degree in Chinese studies at the University of Hawai'i, he owned no car and walked everywhere from 'Āina Haina to Mānoa to Waikīkī. His poems and a rare photo or two document his appearance then: bald-headed and bearded or long and 'ehu (reddish-tinged, sun-bleached) haired—his clothes tattered and soaked in sweat. Nearly every poem from this section includes the line "down on the sidewalk in Waikiki," and with each piece Westlake cunningly puns on the word "down" and its multiplicity of meanings. Sadly, over 25 years later, Westlake's images still haunt Waikīkī: innumerable noisy tourists, ubiquitous concrete and cracking asphalt amidst neutered coconut trees, anonymous hookers, greedy businessmen, indifferent clerks, corrupt cops, lost hippies, pseudo-surfers, confused Jesus freaks, feral cats, rats and the homeless, particularly those of Hawaiian ancestry.[20]

Down on The Sidewalk in Waikiki[21]

No need feel sorry
    for the crippled man
    down on the sidewalk
      —in Waikiki

There are a lot more crippled
    minds
      limping around,
    feel sorry for them!

Some eight years after he had compiled, then filed away, this 73-page typescript, unpublished collection, Westlake published an article in the *Pacific Islands Monthly*, in which he wrote:

> The Pacific Island leaders are not about to fall for the illusory promises of the American Dream. Nobody knows better than they do that progress in the wrong direction is not progress at all. They are not so naive as not to know the real reasons why America is so suddenly interested in their affairs. It is clear as the ocean surrounding their islands that the United States wants something, in fact, needs something from them now desperately. And that something is obvious: instant windfall profits from massive over-development; a place to store and dump nuclear garbage; greedy exploitation of ocean resources; and, most of all, forward strategic military outposts.
>
> Nor are the Pacific leaders about to be fooled by Hawaii's role in the American scheme. They are not so blind as not to see Hawaii as it really

is: a "super-colonised" U.S.[,] barren, physically over-developed and over-populated, economically dependent on tourism and the U.S. military, and spiritually dead. They see Hawaii as a place where indigenous peoples' traditions and heritage have been raped and bastardized, crushed and demolished, all in the name of Progress and the American Dream. Hawaii is no "role model" for Pacific Island territories and emerging nations to imitate. If anything, it's an example to avoid.[22]

Longer poems pepper the text prior to, but especially after, his "Down on the Sidewalk in Waikiki" series; these narrative pieces juxtapose sharply with his short poems, revealing, in autobiographical style, diary-like details and metaphors of his life and times. His longer poems are often pedagogic in the philosophical and instructional sense, much like Han Shan's poems, but they are also autobiographically structured and working-class oriented—epiphanies found in the ordinary and commonplace reminiscent of poet Charles Bukowski. Another theme within the text is Westlake's sometimes alarming allusions to personal experiences with poverty and a prevailing sense of impermanence and death.

Westlake's longest poem, the heretofore unpublished "God," was composed in four-line repetitive stanzas and is best read aloud; it is part autobiographical commentary on contradictory messages of purported Christians, hypocritical politicians and preachers, as well as a scathing critique of bourgeois values and attitudes. Here Westlake writes on behalf of the impoverished and downtrodden, documenting suffering and hypocrisy despite vast resources exploited for the benefit of the few. His final stanza in "God" reminds his readers to spiral back to the beginning of this poem, then contemplate between the lines.

True to his poetic philosophy, Westlake's short poems included "everything," whether he was writing about the ordinary, the profane, or criticizing tourism and its deleterious effects upon the Hawaiian people, their culture, their indigenous language and once pristine landscapes. In 1981, Westlake published several short poems from a work in progress titled "Dagger in the Hand of Aloha":

Breadfruit

breadfruit
what's that?

the tourist gasped—
should'a stuffed one
in her face!

Breadfruit is "'*ulu*" in the Hawaiian language, but one of the many mean-
ings of *ulu* (pronounced similarly to '*ulu*, depending on its usage and syn-
tax) is "to grow," and also to be "possessed by a god; inspired by a spirit,
god, ideal, person." Furthermore, '*ulu* is one of Westlake's '*aumakua*, a per-
sonalized family deity or ancestral entity.[23] The tourist in question reacts
to the unusual-looking breadfruit with disdain and surprise. In contrast
to the tourist's perspective, the poet's voice is intolerant, exactly echoing
this tourist's hasty revulsion. The irony lies in the abject meanness evoked
by the poet when, in fact, the tourist and her dollars are supposed to be
welcomed. In this hyperbole, Westlake candidly informs his readers that
he's replacing the "culture of aloha" with impatience and an intolerance
for cultural ignorance.[24] The poem's title is innocuous, but its contents
are devastating. For some readers, this venting is delightfully blasphemous,
even humorous, and for others, deliberately offensive; in sum, the poem
evokes, if not provokes, controversy. In 1978, three years before "Bread-
fruit" was first published, Westlake wrote this letter to the editor:

> I am also sick of hearing the Navy's threats to pull out of Hawaii and relo-
> cate elsewhere. Fine with me. Go, I say. Beat it! Nothing but good can come
> from such a move. Sure our island economy will suffer, but maybe that's
> what we here in Hawaii need. One thing is certain—we will survive.
>
> Throughout history, Hawaiians have considered all their land sacred.
> Americans obviously don't, and never did. So let them take their business
> and bombs, their death, destruction and desecration back to their own
> homeland. Believe me, it will be a long awaited relief, and something I'm
> sure we all could learn to live with.[25]

Westlake's collages and concrete poetry—manipulations of letters,
words, and images that are graphically rendered into visual art—are in-
tegrated, although not chronologically, throughout this collection. Several
of his concrete poems were exhibited in Honolulu galleries in the late
1970s and published worldwide. Significantly, Westlake was the first to in-
tegrate the Hawaiian language into this literary form.[26] Hawaiian words
can have multiple meanings and include homonyms and heteronyms, al-

lowing for the creation of trenchantly witty if not playful concrete poems. Furthermore, traditionally trained Hawaiian poets and composers often employ a compositional device called kaona, "hidden or veiled meaning," a technique that adds exceptional dimensions to poetry, songs, and chants crafted in the Hawaiian language where wordplay, riddling, symbolism, metaphors, allusions, and unique experiences are intricately interwoven. Westlake utilizes such devices within his concrete poetry, an international contemporary movement rooted in Dadaism, futurism, and surrealism, which he brilliantly indigenizes.[27]

His concrete poem "Pupule" means "crazy, insane, reckless, wild." Readers can derive a multitude of different but related Hawaiian words and definitions from the four common letters that are scattered repeatedly on the page, an anagram of clever if not ominous riddling and wordplay. Viewed from a distance, the black-inked, rubber-stamped letters appear to form a circular, perhaps orderly shape, like a wobbly whiffle ball, but when closely examined, there is randomness and an appearance of chaos. This piece often elicits laughter and surprise; however, beyond its apparent and very real humor is an undercurrent frothing with Hawaiian words that underscores madness or insanity, as reflected in the poem's title. This brilliantly constructed concrete poem conceals a vibrant commentary on and critical response to the ravaging effects of the illegal occupation of Hawaiian lands; it also echoes often unstated emotions and feelings of a historically disenfranchised people and culture. One key to the puzzle is the challenge of discovering scores of Hawaiian words created from only four Hawaiian letters: *p, u, l,* and *e* (which sequentially spell a kind of prayer—or non-prayer).[28] Add to that diacriticals ē, ʻē, ū, and ʻū, and the word combinations amplify.[29] The puzzle in this concrete poem lay in the spiderweb of Hawaiian words. Recalling the Greek legend of the Sphinx who guarded the city of Thebes, to not solve the riddle is to die; to unravel the riddle brings life and instant heroism, but the hero's status foreshadows doom and wit's end. Westlake's tragic and sardonic poem, a riddle, if you will, with genuine humor and wit at its core, is built around one Hawaiian word whose letters silently explode into a babble of many Hawaiian words, simultaneously resisting and protesting the marginalization of a viable, ancient classical Hawaiian language, literature, and oral tradition—madness and tragedy, indeed.

In another concrete poem featuring the Hawaiian word "HULI," Westlake uses large block lettering, inked black, and has literally turned the word over. The definitions of *huli* include: "to turn, reverse; to curl over, as a breaker; to change, as an opinion or manner of living; to look for, search, explore, seek, study; search, investigation; scholarship"; "section, as of a town, place, or house"; "taro top, as used for planting; shoot, as of wauke"; "trump or winning card"; "same as *hului*, bag net."[30] In an editorial, "The Separatist View," published in the *Honolulu Advertiser*, on November 23, 1979, he predicted:

> As inevitable mangos ripen and rot, the time will ultimately arrive when the case of the illegal overthrow of the Hawaiian monarchy by the United States of America will have to be tried in court, be it U.S. federal court or one from the United Nations.
>
> As more and more seeds of separatism take root, deepen and spread, the return of a sovereign Hawaiian nation appears less and less far-fetched.[31]

Two years later, on September 1981, in a detailed *Honolulu Star-Bulletin* editorial titled "The Overthrow of the Hawaiian Monarchy," Westlake wrote: "And in a long dispatch sent to [U.S. Secretary of State John W.] Foster that same day, [U.S. Minister John L.] Stevens made his most memorable statement: 'The Hawaiian pear is now fully ripe, and this is the golden hour for the United States to pluck it.'"[32] Just as in 1893 when the descendants of missionaries and their "Committee of Safety" overthrew the Hawaiian monarchy, so too Westlake advocated a complete turning over of the present government. Backed by an international poetry movement and over a hundred years of Hawaiian resistance to the theft of their sovereignty, this piece exemplifies poetic minimalism created by one whose choice of weapons was not the brandished sword, machine gun, or terrorist bomb, but a single, indigenous Hawaiian word: *huli.*

Westlake's concrete poem "Manifesto" (for concrete poetry), is a playfully graphic work (pun intended), layered with commentary and wittily snubbing the literary status quo. Alive with urgency, "Manifesto" comes to life particularly when read aloud—yelling, whispering, laughing, speaking each line. The lone, repeated Chinese character "Wu," also pronounced "Mu" in Japanese, visually leaps from the page to a sonically perceived sound reminiscent of a cow lowing, echoic of an Orwellian protest chant, with Chairman Mao Tse-tung's words immediately following: "'Millionaires will lose millions'/'Revolution is no dinner party.'" "Wu" signifies the void, nothingness, emptiness—an ideogram utilized by Taoist poets, philosophers, and adepts worldwide. Grasping the concept of "Wu" signifies expansive, seemingly paradoxical understanding. In one stanza early in the poem he exclaims:

> Language the missionaries taught us was broken glass.
> Our tongues are still bleeding.

Born in 1947, Westlake is from a generation of both Hawaiians and non-Hawaiians that was, for the most part, severed from one of Hawai'i's two official languages—Hawaiian. An indigenous renaissance cannot fully blossom without a massive revitalization of its language, and "Manifesto" is this Hawaiian poet's volcanic eruption in the face of devastating cultural hypocrisy:

> Kiss the lyrical poets, bite off and spit out their tongues!
> Hug the intellectual poets, twist and snap off their heads!
> Fondle the technical poets, lick and suck out their eyeballs!

"Got enough TNT? Enough grenades? Try blow up a concrete poet: / Like blowing up air!" When he declares, in the same breath, that "'Literature is in constant need of rebarbarization,'" Westlake is not only quoting from yet another concrete poem that he had published, but insisting on the restoration of his "barbarous" indigenous tongue and Hawaiian literature, reminding his readers, via Mao Tse-tung, that "revolution is no dinner party." Indeed, turning the tables on an occupied, colonized Hawai'i requires more than polemics; "Manifesto" is picture-book satire, a complex, imaginative recipe for overthrowing the status quo.

Westlake's final years found him engaged in intense research, crafting articles supporting Hawaiian sovereignty, challenging geothermal development in Puna, testifying against a proposed satellite missile launching base in Ka'ū on the island of Hawai'i, and, when the occasion called for it, creating more concrete poetry.[33]

Without Mei-Li's efforts, much of Westlake's poetry would have remained inaccessible to us. Not all of his work appears here, of course, including his translations and notes that have yet to be compiled or examined. Future editions should follow, but as Mei-Li says, "This is enough for now."

If Westlake had been alive today in 2007, he would have been 60 years old. His poetry stands singular in its scope and breadth; and though he died when he was only 36, he will one day be regarded with affection as an "old master." With ever-changing tides and in centuries yet to unfold, "an immortal poet" he is and will be!

Richard Hamasaki
Kāne'ohe, 2007

Acknowledgments

Mahalo piha to Mark Hamasaki for his painstaking book design of *Westlake* and for his photographs; to Kapulani Landgraf for printing Mark's photos as well as shooting several images of Westlake's concrete poems; and to Ward Westlake, Bo Hunter, Russell Kokubun, and Myron Wong for sharing their precious memories and insights. Deep appreciation is also extended to Paul Lyons, Dennis Kawaharada, Rodney Morales, and Holly Yamada for their incisive editorial suggestions and reconstructions regarding my introduction and afterword.

Special acknowledgment must be made to all who contributed to and helped with our thirtyninehotel, October 20, 2006, Westlake book-publishing fund-raiser. We not only raised the required funds for the University of Hawai'i Press; additional donations made to Kuleana 'Ōiwi Press helped to establish the Wayne Kaumualii Westlake Book Series. Also, *mahalo ā nui loa* to the Charles and Beatrice Parrent Fund and each of the fund's committee members for their encouragement and support during my sabbatical leave from Kamehameha Schools in 2002–2003. And *mahalo* to Lee Tonouchi and Masako Ikeda. Lee, after interviewing me for *Hybolics* (no. 2), met with Masako of the University of Hawai'i Press, with whom he shared copies of Westlake's published poetry photocopied from the Hawaiian/Pacific collection at UHM. They, along with my brother Mark, strongly urged me to contact Mei-Li Siy, Wayne's literary executor.

Finally, Mei-Li's permission to publish Westlake is a gift to the world, and her entrusting me with Wayne's manuscripts is beyond words.

Notes

Introduction

1. Westlake's full name is taken directly from his typescript resumé.
2. His chapbook was titled *It's Okay If You Eat Lots of Rice* (West Lafayette, IN: High/Coo Press, 1979) and cofeatured illustrations by Kailua (Oʻahu) artist Kimie Takahashi.
3. Mei-Li Siy, whose married name is Cope, wrote the following, included in the large box of Westlake's manuscripts that she sent to me from Kona, Hawaiʻi: "I hope this is enough to get you started. You'll be amazed [at] the amount of unpublished poetry there is. Take good care of them. I trust them in your hands. I found it somewhat difficult in letting go of them. Part—because Wayne's not here to ask his permission. The other, oh well—you'll understand when you begin reading them" (June 10, 2001).
4. Per phone conversation with Ward Westlake, July 18, 2003.
5. Frank and Elsa Westlake were married on October 10, 1942, as described in the *Honolulu Advertiser:* "In a setting of white ginger and lighted tapers, Miss Elsa Marjorie Reichardt, daughter of Mr. and Mrs. [Jane Miller] W. C. Reichardt of Lahaina, Maui, became the bride of Frank Raymond Westlake, son of Mr. and Mrs. F. W. Westlake of Lihue, Kauai. The Rev. Mr. Henry P. Judd performed the ceremony at the Church of the Crossroads on October 10. The bride's uncle, M. E. Miller, gave her in marriage. Business affairs prevented her father's attendance" (October 24, 1942). Both Frank and Elsa Westlake graduated from the University of Hawaiʻi, and Elsa earned her master's degree from Columbia University. Much later, they would divorce.
6. See Mary Kawena Pukui et al., eds., *Nānā i ke Kumu*, vol. 1 (Honolulu: Hui Hānai, 1972), 96–100, regarding inoa, the personal name: "Giving names to commemorate events in the lives of aliʻi could have been a risky business. Nobody took another's name without permission, and names of royalty were especially kapu.... Both cases show the alternate ways tradition provides for handling kapu names. Mrs. Pukui describes them: 'You can ʻoki [sever] the name and take a new one, or you can ʻoki the kapu and keep the name.... My name isn't supposed to be given away. My name is for me. But people are always naming babies after me, so I have many namesakes. I don't want any of them hurt if there's any kapu that goes with my name. So I pray, 'Since so-and-so named this child for me, then

please do me the favor to 'oki the kapu and bless the name. Whatever kapu there is, bring it back to me, but don't let it bother the child.' This prayer is called pule ho'onoa, 'prayer to free.'"

7. Westlake once shared with me that his interest in poetry began in high school when one of his teachers introduced him to Dadaism.

8. I learned that Wayne and Bo—who was from Wahiawā and had attended Princeton University on a full scholarship—participated in many book-related conversations on Asian and European philosophers (from Chuang-Tzu to Nietzsche) in the late 1960s and into the 1970s. Thoroughly versed in Chinese poetry and philosophy as he was, Westlake's reading included Catullus, Cocteau, Bukowski, Patchen, Ginsberg, Snyder, Ferlinghetti, Pound, Kerouac, William Carlos Williams, Kobo Abe, Kenzaburo Oe, Osamu Dazai, Guillaume Apollinaire, Charles Baudelaire, Henry Miller, Takuboku Ishikawa, Issa, Buson, Bashō, Shinkichi Takahashi, Li Po, Han Shan, Lao Tzu, Mao Tse-tung, Ho Chi Minh, Langston Hughes, Ralph Ellison, Malcolm X, James Baldwin, Amiri Baraka, Che Guevera, Gabriel García Márquez, S. N. Haleole, Keaulumoku, G. W. Kahiolo, David Malo, Samuel Mānaiakalani Kamakau, John Dominis Holt, Albert Wendt, and a host of others.

9. Translator Thomas Cleary writes that the "earliest historical Taoist text is attributed to a minister of the founder of the old Shang-Yin dynasty in the 18th century B.C." *The Essential Tao* (San Francisco: Harper 1991), 123–124.

10. In *Poetry East-West* (Honolulu: Friends of the East-West Center, 1975).

11. In December 1973, Westlake earned his B.A., with honors, in Chinese studies from the University of Hawai'i, Mānoa.

12. See notes in *Spider Bone Diaries, Poems and Songs* (Honolulu: University of Hawai'i Press, 2001) for more details regarding some of the dynamics and personalities behind *Seaweeds and Constructions* (1976–1984).

13. Beginning with this period, Westlake wrote numerous letters to the editor, editorials, and articles that addressed land struggles, the illegal overthrow of the Hawaiian monarchy, and subsequent occupation of the Hawaiian nation; see his Bibliography.

14. On December 31, 1968, Wayne published a short satirical comment in the *Honolulu Advertiser* called "Realizing God," and later, on March 27, 1969, wrote: "I am amazed by the sick humor used by individuals opposing the nationwide grape boycott. In particular I am speaking of John E. White ('Peeling' the Grape Boycotters 3/21/69) and the members of the Young Americans for Freedom." Wayne concludes his pithy six-paragraph piece: "So, as you eat your grapes Mr. White, YAF members, and others, remember what you are doing—hastening the death of the now starving children

of these striking grape pickers. If this is a joke to you, then I feel sorry for you because, to you, life must be a joke." These, as far as I could gather, are samples of his earliest published writing.

15. Read Rodney Morales' account in *Ho'iho'i Hou, A Tribute to George Helm and Kimo Mitchell*, in *Bamboo Ridge*, no. 22 (Spring 1984), and Walter Ritte, Jr., and Richard Sawyer's *Na Mana'o Aloha o Kaho'olawe* (Honolulu: Aloha 'Āina o na Kupuna, 1978).

16. A former girlfriend of Westlake's once confided that he literally wept, deeply grieving Helm and Mitchell's deaths.

17. This collection was reprinted in *Seaweeds and Constructions*, no. 5 (1978) and dedicated to George Helm and Kimo Mitchell, lost at sea, March 6, 1977; this same compilation of student compositions later appeared in other periodicals and publications. In 1984, two months after Westlake died, the Hawai'i State House of Representatives passed a resolution honoring the memory of Wayne K. Westlake, noting his "'leadership, persistence and out-spokenness in the protection of the Hawaii environment and culture,' his involvement in literary programs in the state and his accomplishments as a writer and Chinese scholar" (*Hawaii Tribune-Herald* [Hilo], March 21, 1984).

18. See the *Hawaii Observer*, no. 116, November 17, 1977, titled "Behind Bars, An Interview with Richard Sawyer and Walter Ritte, Jr." Westlake's questions are incisive and uncompromising, especially in light of Helm and Mitchell's disappearance in February 1977. Sawyer and Ritte were jailed for five months, then released one month earlier than expected for "good behavior."

19. In Kathy Titchen's "30 Hawaiian Petroglyphs Are Discovered on Kahoolawe," *Honolulu Star-Bulletin*, July 18, 1979, F9.

20. Examples can be found in *Haku Mele O Hawaii*, Office of Instructional Services/General Education Branch, vol. 2 (Honolulu: Department of Education, January 1977), and in "Kahoolawe: Chants, Legends, Poems, Stories by Children of Maui," in *Seaweeds and Constructions*, no. 5 (1978).

21. In early 1980, we were asked by then Ethnic Studies director Franklin Odo to develop a course on the multiethnic literature of Hawai'i, ES-370. At the time, certain professors and administrators, one in particular from the University of Hawai'i at Mānoa's English department, insisted that the course be titled "Ethnic Writings of Hawai'i." Despite vigorous protests on our part, we were told either to accept the denigrating title or the course would not be approved; bitter, but determined to teach Hawai'i's literature at the university, we acquiesced. ES-370 is now officially entitled "Ethnic Literature of Hawai'i" and is taught by Rodney Morales, Candace

Fujikane, Kuualoha Hoomanawanui, Gary Pak, and others from the University of Hawai'i English department.

22. In *Haku Mele o Hawaii,* vol. 2, January 1977.

23. See Westlake's Bibliography. In 1981, New York publisher and poet John Laughlin of New Directions Press anthologized three of Westlake's innovative concrete poems, two of which were originally published in *Seaweeds and Constructions,* no. 6 (1979).

24. Letter from WW to RH, dated September 10, 1981; titles appear verbatim.

25. See "No Peace among Writers" (letter to the editor), *Honolulu Star-Bulletin,* January 13, 1979, and his "A Thousand Poems," in which he writes: "late at night / all alone / like a treasure chest / I open my suitcase / full of neatly / piled poems."

26. "Hawaiian Artists' Plight" (letter to the editor), *Honolulu Advertiser,* April 17, 1980.

27. Thanks to Crocombe, Subramani, and Wendt, the South Pacific Creative Arts Society and Mana Publications, based in Fiji, supported us ('Elepaio Press) with much needed funds—about $2000.00—so we could produce both "A Pacific Islands Collection" (1983, 1984) and the Hawai'i edition for *Mana, A South Pacific Journal of Language and Literature* vol. 6, no. 1 (1981). Ironically, we had received significantly more assistance and encouragement from the SPCAS and Mana Publications than from our own State Foundation on Culture in the Arts (SFCA), despite the latter's multimillion-dollar mandate to assist the arts in Hawai'i.

28. In 1983, we printed 500 copies of the first edition of *Seaweeds and Constructions,* no. 7, then reprinted another 500 copies after Westlake's death in 1984. On a shoestring budget, my limited resources allowed for only very small print runs from 1976 to 1984: *Seaweeds and Constructions:* no. 1 (150 copies); no. 2 (200 copies); no. 3 (300 copies, funded in part by the SFCA); no. 4 (500 copies); no. 5 (500 copies); no. 6 (approximately 1,000 copies).

Afterword

1. Westlake states in the Preface that he began writing poetry when he was 16, but he burned five years of his writing and regretted this loss.

2. Westlake rarely used Hawaiian diacriticals; however, some diacriticals were added posthumously, as in "My Dog Is Panting." With few exceptions (such as occasional typos found in his original manuscripts), Westlake's titles and poems appear verbatim.

3. Wayne's childhood friends Russell Kokubun and Myron Wong shared many memories with me on January 21, 2003, and we met again later, with another of Westlake's close friends, Bo Hunter, on February 3, 2003;

both meetings lasted nearly four hours. Russell and I both recall Wayne saying this to us, on separate occasions, many years ago.

4. See Westlake's poem "No One Understands the Sea" where he documents, early in his career, receiving some 33 rejection slips. Some 30 years after his death, I was amazed and stunned while reading through packets of poems that he had hidden away, work that should have been published in his lifetime. Alas, these opportunities had slipped away, especially because of Wayne's magnanimous nature: he was always more interested in seeing other local authors in print, Hawaiians and non-Hawaiians alike.

5. "Send Him a Pineapple or Two" and "My Suitcase Full of Teeth" were recorded live at a University of Hawai'i Ethnic Studies forum on Hawai'i's literature, circa 1981, but were incompletely recorded because one side of the cassette tape was full and had to be removed by the audio technician, and then reversed in the middle of Westlake's reading.

6. Compare Westlake's "On top Puff-Rice Mountain I meet Tu Fu! / wearing a bamboo rain-hat in the noonday sun" with translator Sam Hamill's version (reprinted from *Crossing the Yellow River: Three Hundred Poems from the Chinese*): "I met Tu Fu on a mountaintop / in August when the sun was hot. / Under the shade of his big straw hat." In 1996, David Hinton translated Li Po's poem "Teasing Tu Fu": "Here on the summit of Fan-k'o Mountain, it's Tu Fu / under a midday sun sporting his huge farmer's hat." The first line of Westlake's translation mostly consists of monosyllabic words and includes two spondaic feet, with one trochaic foot followed by two more spondees. His translation cleverly attempts to match the English with Li Po's original poem rendered in Chinese ideograms: four lines, five characters per line, and one tone per syllable, per character.

7. See the Bibliography for references to other published translations by Westlake.

8. One of Westlake's termite-eaten manuscripts consists of 34 typescript poems, some with written revisions. Although not dated, one poem indicates that Westlake was 27 years old at the time (circa 1974).

9. See Yasuichi Awakawa, *Zen Painting* (Tokyo: Kodansha International, 1970; 1974).

10. Haiku poet Teishitsu (d. 1673) wrote: "Here I am among the flowers! / I hear people laughing / In the spring mountains" and "Let's go up to Saga, / You seagulls, / And eat trout!" in R. H. Blythe, *A History of Haiku*, vol. 1 (Tokyo: Hokuseido Press, 1963), 71. Gary Snyder, in *Rip Rap*, describes Han Shan (7th c. A.D.) via Lu Ch'iu-Yin, governor of T'ai Prefecture: "No one knows just what sort of man Han-Shan was. At the temple lived Shih-te, who ran the dining hall. He sometimes saved leftovers for Han-Shan, hiding them in a bamboo tube. Han-Shan would come

and carry it away; walking the long veranda, calling and shouting happily, talking and laughing to himself. Once the monks followed him, caught him, and made fun of him. He stopped, clapped his hands, and laughed greatly—Ha Ha!—for a spell, then left"; Gary Snyder, *Rip Rap, and Cold Mountain Poems* (San Francisco: Four Seasons Foundation, 1958; 1965), 33. Buson wrote in the 18th century: "Listening to the waterfalls / From here and there: / The young leaves!" Blythe, *History of Haiku,* vol. 1, 245.

11. From Santōka's August 19, 1940, diary entry in Blythe, *History of Haiku,* vol. 2 (Tokyo: Hokuseido Press, 1964), 175.

12. Santōka also wrote: "I do not believe in a future world. I deny the past. I believe entirely in the present. We must employ our whole body and soul in this eternal moment. I believe in the universal spirit, but the spirit of any particular man I reject. Each creature comes from the Whole, and goes back to it. From this point of view we may say that life is an approaching; death is a returning" (ibid., 175). Another 15th-century haiku poet wrote: "Its name all unknown, / A weed flowers / By the side of a stream" (53). Westlake was a devotee of Blythe's anthologies and his commentaries on Japanese haiku poetry and often consulted Blythe's texts when translating his own versions of Issa.

13. The following is a good example of a traditional ʻōlelo noʻeau that West-lake's poetics would reflect: "O ka kāʻule nehe o ka lau lāʻau, / he hāwa-nawana ia i ka poʻe ola. The rustling of falling leaves is / like a whisper to the living." In Mary Kawena Pukui's *ʻŌlelo Noʻeau* (No. 2404) (Honolulu: Bishop Museum Press, 1983).

14. See Ellen Kehoʻohiwaokalani Wright Prendergast's "Mele ʻAi Pohaku, or Stone-eating Song," also called "Mele Aloha Aina (Patriots' Song)," and "Kaulana nā Pua," in Samuel H. Elbert and Noelani Mahoe, *Nā Mele O Hawaiʻi Nei* (Honolulu: University of Hawaiʻi Press, 1970).

15. "The Sacred Struggle for Land" (letter to the editor), *Honolulu Star-Bulletin,* October 25, 1980.

16. In Elbert and Mahoe, *Nā Mele O Hawaiʻi Nei,* 64.

17. Westlake's unpublished manuscript "Down on the Sidewalk in Waikiki" consists of 73 typed pages on 8½ x 11-inch paper with extensive hand-written revisions on selected poems; it is wrapped with yellow and silver paper with kapa patterns and hand-bound with yellow twine. A later manuscript includes the inscription "Poems by Kamalii Kahakai" and is dedicated "to the Kahuna of Waikiki." In 1982, poet and editor Joe Balaz published a single poem from this series in his literary magazine *Ramrod,* titled "Down on the Sidewalk in Waikiki."

18. For a similar reading of tourism in Hawaiʻi, see Haunani-Kay Trask's *Light in the Crevice Never Seen* (Corvallis, OR: Calyx Books, 1994; 1999) and her

Night Is a Sharkskin Drum (Honolulu: University of Hawai'i Press, 2002). Trask's polemics are cunning and multilayered. Like Westlake's poems from "Down on the Sidewalk in Waikiki" (1972–1973) and "Dagger in the Hand of Aloha" (1981), one of Trask's strategies is to discomfort readers and engage them in hard-hitting perspectives of the oppressed, especially if the oppressors happen to be tourists—"innocent" perhaps, but still part and parcel of Hawai'i's pervasive agencies of exploitation and profiteering.

19. See the Papua Pocket Poets series (1967–1975), affiliated with the University of Papua New Guinea. Soon after the University of Papua New Guinea opened in 1966, a dynamic, far-reaching art and literary movement in Oceania emerged. Indigenous authors elsewhere, like Maori poet Hone Tuwhare, began publishing in English in the 1950s and 1960s, and Hawaiian writer John Dominis Holt published *On Being Hawaiian* in 1964 and contemporary short stories in English and Pidgin, *Today Ees Sad-dy Night and Other Stories,* in 1965. Unfortunately, communication regarding various emerging literary movements within vast Oceania, even within smaller Hawai'i, was lacking largely due to insular, colonial educational systems and its narrowly focused media. See also "A Pacific Islands Collection," *Seaweeds and Constructions,* no. 7 (1983, 1984), which Westlake coedited with me subsquent to Colleen Kimura's gift of copies of the Papua Pocket Poets series along with chapbooks published by Mana Publications and the South Pacific Creative Arts Society—collected by Colleen when she worked in Fiji with the Peace Corps in the early 1980s.

20. Regarding Westlake's caustic honesty in "Down on the Sidewalk in Waikiki," consider these lines from Han Shan: "Cold Mountain speaks these words / as if he were a madman / he tells people what he thinks / thus he earns their wrath / but a straight mind means straight words / a straight mind holds nothing back / crossing the River of Death / who's that jabbering fool / the road to the grave is dark / and karma holds the reins," in Red Pine's *The Collected Songs of Cold Mountain* (No. 234) (Port Townsend, WA: Copper Canyon Press, 2000), 199.

21. In his lifetime, Westlake published only this one particular poem from his "Down on the Sidewalk in Waikiki" typescripts.

22. "Pacific Leaders Aren't Blind," *Pacific Islands Monthly* 51, no. 12 (December 1980).

23. Wayne shared this information about his 'aumakua with me around 1980, when we were co-teaching at the University of Hawai'i, Mānoa.

24. See Pukui and Elbert's definition of aloha 'ino: "too bad, what a shame"; the word 'ino has many negative connotations, including "wicked, immoral, sinful, unwholesome, unclean, bad, vicious, evil, unprincipled;

hate, sin, decomposition"; and aloha 'ole: "pitiless, merciless, ungrateful, without love or affection." *Hawaiian Dictionary* (Honolulu: University of Hawai'i Press, 1986), 101; 21.

25. "'Go Away, Navy'" (letter to the editor), *Honolulu Advertiser*, July 24, 1978.

26. In the introduction to her book *Concrete Poetry: A World View* (Bloomington: Indiana University Press, 1968), Mary Ellen Solt was careful to avoid any simple definition of this contemporary genre of modern poetry:

> The term "concrete poetry" is now being used to refer to a variety of innovations and experiments following World War II which are revolutionizing the area of the poem on a global scale and enlarging its possibilities for expression and communication ... the concrete poet is concerned with establishing his linguistic materials in a new relationship to space (the page or its equivalent) and / or to time (abandoning old linear measure). Put another way this means the concrete poet is concerned with making an object to be perceived rather than read.... Concrete poets, then, are united in their efforts to make objects or compositions of sounds from particular materials. They are disunited on the questions of semantics: some insisting upon the necessity for poetry to remain within the communication area of semantics, others convinced that poetry is capable of transmitting new and other kinds of information—purely esthetic information. (Solt 1968:7)

27. An earlier analysis of Westlake's poetry can be found in my University of Hawai'i (Mānoa) Center for Pacific Islands Studies M.A. thesis, "Singing in Their Genealogical Trees: The Emergence of Contemporary Hawaiian Poetry in English, Dana Naone Hall, Wayne Kaumualii Wayne, Joseph P. Balaz" (1989).

28. "Pule" has many meanings: "prayer, magic spell, incantation, blessing, grace, church service ... to pray, worship, say grace, ask a blessing, cast a spell." Mary Kawena Pukui and Samuel H. Elbert (Honolulu: University of Hawai'i Press, 1986), 353.

29. Go to http://wehewehe.org and enter, for example: *u, uu, uuu, ule, pu, puu, pupu, pule, e, ee, eee*, etc. Scores of Hawaiian words can be constructed from these four letters along with two diacriticals, the 'okina and kahakō.

30. In Pukui and Elbert, *Hawaiian Dictionary*, 1986.

31. "The Separatist View" (editorial), *Honolulu Advertiser*, November 23, 1979.

32. See Westlake's lengthy editorial, "The Overthrow of the Hawaiian Monarchy," *Honolulu Star-Bulletin,* September 29, 1981.

33. Westlake's last creative work was probably his concrete poem "teaching my dog buddhism" which he had sent to friends in January 1984, approximately one month before his death.

Bibliography of the Publications of
Wayne Edward Kaumualii Miller Westlake

This bibliography was compiled ([1985] 2001–2004) by Mei-Li M. Siy and Richard Hamasaki. Our thanks to Jennifer Dang for photocopying—in the *Honolulu Advertiser* archives—many of Westlake's letters, editorials, and articles that were published in the *Honolulu Advertiser* and the *Honolulu Star-Bulletin* (1968–1983).

Poems (Periodicals)

1975: "A Joke—To Tu Fu." *Chicago Review,* vol. 26, no. 4 (1974; copyright on masthead says 1975).

1976: "Bamboos," "Farmers," "Dead Man," "Woman's Liberation," "Sacred Tortoise," and an untitled poem. Concrete poems. *Seaweeds and Constructions* (Honolulu), no. 1.

1978: "And If Your Mind Had Wings." *Bamboo Ridge* (Honolulu), no. 1, December.

1979: "Half My Face Is Falling Off." Concrete poem typescript. *En Passant* (Wilmington, DE), no. 9.

"One hundred haiku. . . ." Untitled poem in *Modern Haiku* (Madison, WI), vol. 10, no. 3, Autumn.

"Look here, toads . . . ," "Fat toads . . . ," "Poets of Today . . . ," "20 day rain—," "Two cigarettes . . . ," "beer cans. . . ." Six untitled poems. *Outch, International Haiku Magazine* (Tokyo: Gonzui-Sha), vol. 4, no. 1, Spring.

"The ant / I rescued . . . ," "Think 'Paradise' . . . ," "'Damn it . . . ," "Every night . . . ," "Hurry over . . . ," "Saw the butterfly. . . ." Six untitled poems. *Outch, International Haiku Magazine* (Tokyo: Gonzui-Sha), vol. 4, nos. 2 and 3, Autumn.

"For weeds / even . . . ," "Full moon—," "Gonna check. . . ." Three untitled poems. *Portals* (Bellingham, WA), vol. 2, no. 3, November.

"Hawaiians Eat Fish" (concrete poem typescript), "In Praise of Boobs," "O . . ." (untitled concrete poem). Three poems. *Plumbers Ink* (Taos, NM), vol. 2, no. 1; published under pseudonym Edward Kaumualii.

1980: "Haiku all night . . . ," "Fleeting as mango . . . ," "Ancient ruins . . . ," "She loves me . . . ," "Her name over and over." Five untitled poems. *Dragonfly* (Portland, OR), vol. 8, no. 2.

"'make you a deal/mr. fly...,'" "full moon...." Two untitled poems. *Echoes* (Campbell, CA), vol. 2, no. 6.

"Can't/be a hermit/yet...," "One inch long...," "14 days rain—." Three untitled poems. *Northeast* (La Crosse, WI), ser. 3, Winter.

"Native-Hawaiian," "The Tourist," "Koloa Day," "Puaʻa," "Breadfruit," "Kaiulani." Six poems (one reprint). *Ramrod* (Wahiawā), no. 1.

1981: "The Loss of Buddha...." *Frogpond* (New York), vol. 4, no. 2.

"Lolo." Untitled concrete poem; Reprint. *Kaala Art Notes* (Haleʻiwa), no. 4, Summer.

"Deaf-Mute Dancing Girl." *Mana* (Suva, Fiji), vol. 6, no. 1.

"Broken English," "Utopia, Only 10 Hours Old, Already Needed a Fix" (concrete poems); "Must be going crazy—," "Read a whole...," "Bonsai...," "Wish I...," "Kakizome." Seven poems (reprinted). *Ramrod* (Wahiawā), no. 2.

"Manifesto for Concrete Poetry" (reprinted). *Poet* (Madras, India), vol. 23, no. 2, February.

"Hawaiians Eat Fish." Concrete poem typescript. *Poet* (Madras, India), vol. 23, no. 6, June.

"Vitamin C Has Reduced the Pus." Concrete poem typescript. *Poet* (Madras, India), vol. 23, no. 10, October.

"Down on the Sidewalk in Waikiki," "A Hawaiian Boy Speaks Out of Place." *Ramrod* (Wahiawā), no. 3.

1982: "Manifesto for Concrete Poetry," "Literature Is in Need of Rebarbarization," "Pupule." Three concrete poems (reprinted). *Oboe* (San Francisco), no. 5.

1983: "Half My Face Is Falling Off." Concrete poem typescript. *Poet* (Madras, India), vol. 24, no. 2, February.

"White House Jabberwocky," "Oozing." Two concrete poems. *Ramrod* (Wahiawā), no. 4.

1984: "Flawed Intelligence," "Third Eye (collages); "Dogo," "Spit," Concrete poems (two of triptych). *Ramrod* (Wahiawā), no. 5.

1985: "Thank You." Concrete poem (one of triptych); "O Democracy," "Hungry Animals Gnawed the Bones," "Just What the Doctor Ordered," "When Passion Comes." Concrete poems. *Ramrod* (Punaluʻu), no 6.

1986: "Minimal Man" (collage). *Ramrod* (Punaluʻu), no. 7.

Anthologies (Poetry and Prose)

"The Drunken Sage," "The Archer," "The Black Dog." Three poems. *Poetry East-West* (Honolulu), 1975.

"Dragon," "Manifesto for Concrete Poetry," "Half My Face Is Falling Off," "Pupule," "Water" (concrete poetry); "Concrete Poetry and the Chinese Written Character" (prose). *Seaweeds and Constructions, Anthology Hawaii* (Honolulu), no. 6, 1979.

"Vitamin C Has Reduced the Pus," "Pupule" (reprinted), "Half My Face Is Falling Off" (reprinted). Three concrete poems. *New Directions 42* (New York), no. 42, 1981.

"Native-Hawaiian" (reprint), "HBV" [*sic*], "The Tourist" (reprint). Three poems from a work in progress titled "Dagger in the Hand of Aloha." Also "Memorial Day." *Poetry East-West* (Honolulu), 1981.

"A." Concrete poem. *Premier Poets* (Madras, India): *The Seventh Biennial Anthology*, January 1, 1981–December 31, 1982.

Translations (Periodicals)

"Greedy men love to gather Wealth ... ," "Pigs eat dead man's meat. . . ." Two poems by Han Shan. *Tantalus* (Honolulu), no. 2, Summer 1974.

"Biography of Shih-Te," "Biography of Feng Kan," "Record of Ch'an Master Feng Kan" by Lu Ch'in Yin; "Collected Poems" by Feng Kan." Prose and poetry translations. *Seaweeds and Constructions* (Honolulu), no. 2, November 1976.

"Melting dew ... ," "Autumn evening—," "Living in the city ... ," "One man ... ," "New clothes ... ," "Old age ... ," "For fleas, too ... ," "Winter—," "Weeping willow ... ," "Clear cold water ... ," "Soft. . . ." Eleven untitled poems by Issa. *Cicada* (Toronto), vol. 3, 1979.

"For fleas too ... ," "Soft willow ... ," "Like an ancient Immortal. . . ." Three untitled poems by Issa. *Hawaii Review* (Honolulu), no. 10, Spring/Fall 1980.

Translations (Anthologies)

"Bamboo shoots ... ," "Melting dew—," "In this World ... ," "It's a Dew-drop World," "In a dream ... ," "One man ... ," "New clothes ... ," "Autumn evening—," "Two cranes eating ... ," "Few snow flakes ... ," "Living in the city ... ," "Beggar in the rain—," "In silence ... ," "Only the birds ... ," "Old age. . . ." Fifteen untitled translations of Issa. *Poetry East-West* (Honolulu: Friends of the East-West Center), 1975.

"As when man meets a Demon ... ," "An old man marries a young girl ... ," "I only got one coat ... ," "I'll teach you something about Fate ... ," "Away from home ten-thousand miles ... ," "Buddhist monks don't hold the Precepts ... ," "Cold Mountain Master ... ," "Days on end I'm always drunk ... ," "Not really walking the true straight way ... ," "Footprints of the Ancients left on thousand / year old stones. . . ." Ten untitled translations of Han Shan. *Poetry East-West* (Honolulu: Friends of the East-West Center), 1975.

"Greedy men love to gather wealth . . . ," "An old man marries a young girl . . . ,"
"When you meet a demon man. . . ." Three untitled poems of Han Shan.
Talk Story, An Anthology of Hawaii's Local Writers (Honolulu: Petro-
nium Press/Talk Story, Inc.), 1978.

Edited Works

"Wahine O Hawaii." *Seaweeds and Constructions* (Honolulu), no. 4, December
1977.
Haku Mele O Hawaii. Coedited with Dana Naone. Office of Instructional Ser-
vices, Department of Education (Honolulu), vol. 5, October 1978.
Mana, A South Pacific Journal of Language and Literature (Hawaii issue). Coed-
ited with Richard Hamasaki in collaboration with Mana Publications,
the South Pacific Creative Arts Society, *Seaweeds and Constructions*
(Honolulu and Suva) and 'Elepaio Press, vol. 6, no. 1, 1981.
"A Pacific Islands Collection." Coedited with Richard Hamasaki. *Seaweeds and
Constructions* (Honolulu), no. 7, 1983. Reprinted in 1984.

Articles and Compilations (Literary)

"Chinese Imagery." *Haku Mele O Hawaii*, Office of Instructional Services,
Department of Education (Honolulu), vol. 2, October 1977.
"'City'/'Country'—Poetry on Kauai." *Haku Mele O Hawaii*, Office of Instruc-
tional Services, Department of Education (Honolulu), vol. 5, October
1978.
Born Pidgin. (Honolulu), 1979. Self-published.
Kahoolawe—Chants, Legends, Poems Stories by Children of Maui. (Honolulu),
1977. Self-published. Reprinted in *Seaweeds and Constructions*, no. 5,
1978; partial reprint in *The Beast* (London, 1984); reprinted in *Ho'iho'i
Hou. Bamboo Ridge* (Honolulu), vol. 22, Spring 1984.

Chapbook

It's Okay If You Eat Lots of Rice. (Twenty-five pages with woodcuts by Kimie
Takahashi). (West Lafayette, IN: High/Coo Press), no. 5, 1979.

Other Articles (Selected)

"Realizing God" (letter to the editor). *Honolulu Star-Bulletin*, December 31,
1968.
"'Sick Grape Humor" (letter to the editor). *Honolulu Advertiser*, March 27,
1969.
"Behind Bars, An Interview with Richard Sawyer and Walter Ritte, Jr." *The
Hawaii Observer*, no. 116, November 17, 1977.
"Kaho'olawe Mana'o." *The Hawaii Observer*, no. 117, December 1, 1977.

"Changing Manoa." *The Hawaii Observer,* no. 121, February 9, 1978.

"Pidgin in Schools" (editorial). *Honolulu Star-Bulletin,* June 3, 1978.

"'Go Away, Navy'" (letter to the editor). *Honolulu Advertiser,* July 24, 1978.

"No Peace among Writers" (letter to the editor). *Honolulu Star-Bulletin,* January 13, 1979.

"Kahoolawe Nuclear Plans" (letter to the editor). *Honolulu Star-Bulletin,* March 31, 1979.

"Kahoʻolawe, Hawaiians Are Also an Endangered Species" (letter to the editor) and selected poems from "Kahoolawe—Chants, Legends, Poems Stories by Children of Maui." *The Beast* (London), no. 3, October–November 1979.

"The Separatist View" (editorial). *Honolulu Advertiser,* November 23, 1979.

"Poetry amid Poverty" (letter to the editor). *Honolulu Star-Bulletin,* December 5, 1979.

"Hawaiian Artists' Plight" (letter to the editor). *Honolulu Advertiser,* April 17, 1980.

"The Overthrow of the Hawaiian Monarchy (editorial). *Honolulu Star-Bulletin,* September 29, 1980.

"The Sacred Struggle for Land" (letter to the editor). *Honolulu Star-Bulletin,* October 25, 1980.

"Pacific Leaders Aren't Blind." *Pacific Islands Monthly,* vol. 51, no. 12, December 1980.

"Viewpoint" (editorial on Space Services Inc. and satellite launching in Kaʻū, Hawaiʻi). *Hawaii Tribune-Herald,* September 3, 1982.

"Big Island Space Site Opposed" (editorial). *Honolulu Star-Bulletin,* September 30, 1982.

"A Threat to Hawaiian Homes Land Use." *The Native Hawaiian,* vol. 6, no. 12, November 1982.

"Hawaiians Do Not Want SSI" (editorial). *Hawaii Tribune-Herald,* December 30, 1982.

"Rockets for Profit at South Pt. (Kaʻu Opposition Stands Ready to Resist)." *Ka Huliau,* July–August, 1983.

Westlake's Unpublished Manuscripts (in Order of Appearance in This Collection)

The entries in this section are drawn from unpublished manuscripts from which some poems were selected to appear in this book. Not included here are several other unpublished manuscripts from which no poems were selected. Facsimiles of the termite-eaten poems are undated, although there is a reference to Westlake's age, 27, which would indicate that the typescript manuscript was probably produced in 1974. The experience of reading through Westlake's unpublished manuscripts is very accurately captured by Mei-Li (see note 3 to the Introduction). All unpublished manuscripts have been organized and archived for Mei-Li.

University of Oregon notebook [C]: begins with "wayne westlake (you ask?)," circa 1971–1972.

"Silence in Waimanalo Destroyed": contains handwritten poems on 64 loose pages of various sizes, plus two University of Hawai'i blue books of handwritten poems, circa 1971–1972.

University of Oregon notebook [A]: "Kyoku—crazy poems": 49 pages, on 8½ x 11 inch paper, of handwritten poems, front and back, with 33 loose handwritten and typed loose pages inserted in the notebook, circa 1971/2–1973.

Maple Leaf Notebook: 6½ x 8 inch spiral notebook with a brown cover with "Art 20 Julynn Wong" inscribed, 24 pages of handwritten pages, front and several on back. Also included are 87 pages of handwritten and typed poems on various sizes of paper, circa late 1972–1973.

University of Oregon notebook [B]: 33 pages of handwritten drafts [front and back sides of most pages], begins: "twenty five billion / another year / that's how old / i feel / isn't it strange / having a birthday?" circa 1971–1973. The bulk of the poems seems to have been written in 1972.

"Frog chorus . . .": 16 typed pages, stapled, 7 x 10 inches, n.d.

"i have heard the bells.": 41 pages of typed poems on loose, 8½ x 11 inch paper, 1974.

"Looks of disbelief . . .": 2 typed pages, stapled, 7 x 10 inches, n.d.

"This night . . .": 22 typed pages, 3 staples, 5.6 x 8.6 inches, n.d.

"Crazy Oyster poems": 21 typed pages, loose, 14 poems in red ink on onion-skin paper; 7 poems typed in black ink, 8.6 x 11 inch bond paper, n.d.

"Spring": 6 typed pages, stapled, 7 x 10 inches, n.d.

"Spencer Butte, Eugene, Oregon poems": 9 individually collected manuscripts, typed and stapled packets, including 13 loose poems, circa late 1960s.

"short poems": 6 typed pages of short poems, 3 staples across the top of 8.6 x 11 inch paper), n.d.

"Drinking Wine—poems of the Tao": typed MS, circa 1971.

"bright mantras": typed MS, circa 1971.

University of Oregon [E]: yellow spiral notebook, 20 pages handwritten, n.d.

"One Thing I Can't Understand": 78 loose, typed pages with 7-page handwritten collection, two different page sizes, circa 1973.

"Gilmore Hall (in rubble)": 30 pages of typed poems on 8½ x 11 inch typing paper, unbound, 1974.

Typescript set of short poems partially destroyed by termites (originals digitally archived), n.d.

"i hear plumeria is poisonous": 36 poems on 8½ x 11 inch typing paper, n.d.

"Punchbowl Poems" [untitled by WW, but includes references to Punchbowl, where he lived temporarily]: includes MS of short poems torn in half and stapled, followed by 30 typed poems on 8½ x 11 inch paper, circa 1974.

"like crossing manoa stream": 55 loose, typed poems, circa 1973.

"Ten-thousand Obis": 49 pages of typed poems on loose, 8½ x 11 inch paper, 1974.

"Well, let's see": MS, 172 pages of handwritten drafts, mostly poems scribbled quickly, many illegible, almost all loose papers in various sizes; begins with a biographical statement. Several poems are circled and appear later in typed manuscripts, circa 1974.

"too much meat!": MS, 26 pages of handwritten drafts, some words illegible, poems written on 8½ x 11 inch lined loose-leaf papers. References to University of Hawai'i professors and religion class date this circa 1973.

"A Translation of Some Scribbled on Scraps/Found in the Pocket of a Madman Gone Insane" [MS A]: 35 pages of typed poems on 8½ x 11 inch white paper, circa 1973.

"DOWN ON THE SIDEWALK IN WAIKIKI" [MS A]: hand-bound with yellow twine wrapped with yellow and silver paper with kapa patterns; 73 pages on 8½ x 11 inch paper with extensive handwritten revisions on selected poems, 1971–1972.

"Down On The Sidewalk In Waikiki" [MS B]: loose typed MS, edited selections: 63 pages on 8½ x 11 inch paper with extensive handwritten revisions on selected poems, 1971–1972.

"God": 21 pages typed with handwritten corrections to text on 8½ x 11 inch paper, circa 1975. [RH corrected occasional typos in original MS.]

"On Having an Intelligent Conversation with My Dog": 3 typed poems from WW to RH, September 10, 1981.

"Teaching My Dog Buddhism": from RH notes for WW's 1984 funeral reception. Hand-stamped version given to me by WW before his death was returned to Mei-Li.